BAKHT SINGH

of

INDIA

Bakht Singh
of
India

The Incredible Account
of a Modern-Day Apostle

T. E. Koshy

Authentic

COLORADO SPRINGS · MILTON KEYNES · HYDERABAD

Authentic Publishing
We welcome your questions and comments.

USA   1820 Jet Stream Drive, Colorado Springs, CO 80921
       www.authenticbooks.com
UK   9 Holdom Avenue, Bletchley, Milton Keynes, Bucks, MK1 1QR
       www.authenticmedia.co.uk
India Logos Bhavan, Medchal Road, Jeedimetla Village,
       Secunderabad 500 055, A.P.

Bakht Singh: The Incredible Account of a Modern-Day Apostle
ISBN-13: 978-1-932805-69-7
ISBN-10: 1-932805-69-9

Cover and interior design: projectluz.com
Cover image used by permission of ChristianAid.org
Editorial team: KJ Larson, Betsy Weinrich

Printed in the United States of America

Contents

Introduction

In the 1930s, India was going through a turbulent time. Her struggle for political independence from Britain was at its zenith under the undisputable leadership of Mahatma Gandhi. He was not only the most popular political leader of India then, but to millions of Indians, he was also their spiritual leader. Influenced by the political and religious power of Mahatma Gandhi and his rising popularity, many Christian leaders and missionaries were reluctant to preach openly Christ as the only Savior and Lord. At that time Christianity in India was at its nadir, plagued by problems from both within and without. Because of its close association with Britain and the West, most non-Christians in India viewed Christianity as foreign and considered it to be non-relevant to India.

Dr. John Webster Grant explained this predicament:

The foreignness of Christianity, in modern India as in medieval Europe, is due not only to our partial understanding of the gospel but also to a strangeness inherent in the gospel itself. Always and everywhere the church has been suspect as an upsetter of traditions and a disturber of folkways. It lives a pilgrim life, calling men to allegiance to the God who measures all the nations in the span of his hand. Religions that grow out of the soil have no problem of indigenization. Their gods are only symbols of the experience and aspirations of a particular culture, and it is inherent in their nature that they do not attempt missionary work among people of other cultures. Only a religion of revelation claiming to bear a message to all men from the living God has difficulty in coming to terms with national customs and ways of life.

Christianity makes a universal claim precisely because it is rooted not in general human knowledge of God but in God's disclosure of himself in specific events that can be located in space and time. . . .

We cannot purge Christianity of its strangeness, for to do so would be to destroy what is distinctive about it. If Christianity were only an idea to be presented or an experience to be shared, we might without much difficulty invite new peoples to clothe the idea or the experience in forms of their own choosing. But the gospel didn't come into the world as a naked idea or as a simple experience. It came embodied in human personality, and in each generation it must be embodied in the living fellowship of the church. Communicating Christianity means more than convincing individuals about Christ or conveying to them an experience of his presence. It means transmitting the life lived and shared by Christ's people, and we cannot transmit that life apart from the forms of thought and worship and organization through which we express it.

In modern times, moreover, the foreignness of Christianity has been greatly aggravated by the close association of missions with an outward movement of European power and the influence that has affected the entire world.[1]

As Dr. Stanley Jones, a prominent American missionary to India, wrote, "But standing amid the shadows of Western civilization, India has seen a Figure who has greatly attracted her. She has hesitated in regard to any allegiance to Him for India has thought that if she took one she would have to take both—Christ and Western civilization went together."[2]

Whenever the church needs a fresh awakening, the Lord raises up someone to call the church back to Himself. Throughout church history, we see this phenomenon: Martin Luther, Nicholas Zinzendorf, John Wesley, George Whitfield, Jonathan Edwards, William Carey, Charles Finney, Hudson Taylor, D.L. Moody to name a few. Bakht Singh of India is one of those God raised up in the twentieth century.

When Bakht Singh first began his work in Karachi in close association with major Protestant denominations, he found many of them lukewarm and unconcerned about the spiritual needs of their congregations. The perpetual practice of caste and class systems was prevalent in the churches. Bakht Singh preached and practiced that all believers were welcome, regardless of the status in life. He emphasized that every believer in Christ whether Brahmin or Dalit (untouchable or outcaste) is equally precious, equally necessary, and equally important in the sight of God. He felt that the caste system was one of the worst evil practices in India and that the problem was deep-rooted, even in the church.

Bakht Singh's vision of the church came as he fasted, prayed, and studied the Word of God. He believed that the church should reflect, radiate, and represent Christ, who is the head of the church. This reflection of Christ in the church needed to be expressed within the cultural and linguistic background of the people so that the "foreignness" of the church might be removed without changing the distinctiveness of the church. This distinctiveness makes the church inclusive of all believers, of all backgrounds, all taking their part in the building up of the local church without having any distinction of clergy or laity.

This led him to plant indigenous churches on the basis of New Testament principles. Bakht Singh's intention was not to Indianize churches but to Christianize churches, where all people, regardless of their caste, color, nationality, and language, could feel at home as they met together. He believed that all born-again believers were part of the universal body of Christ and welcomed all. The church became a place where former Brahmin converts now stooped down and served the converted untouchables who had become part of God's family. The highly educated served the illiterate and vice-versa.

Bakht Singh's life and ministry were unique in many ways. The majority of Indians believed that Christianity was essentially a religion of the West and one could not be a Christian and an Indian at the same time. He made Christianity relevant to the people of India. He helped people see that one could be a Christian and Indian at the same time and regardless of his or her religion, caste, or class could follow the Christ of the New Testament without having to follow Western culture. He demonstrated that the New Testament church-principles transcend time, place, and people and can be applied to people of any culture, country, or language without compromising the Word of God.

Never begging for support, Bakht Singh demonstrated that one could trust God for every need. But he accepted support sent to him by people of their own volition. He taught believers the importance of tithing and encouraged them to give sacrificially. He practiced and preached living in simplicity. Content with what he had, he knew how to live in poverty and in prosperity.

Bakht Singh taught and practiced the importance of partnership in missions where East and West could be united to fulfill the purposes of God. He worked closely with WEC missionaries and Operation Mobilization and attended the Lausanne Congress on World Evangelization in 1974. As time permitted, he attended and participated in the Evangelical Fellowship of India (EFI) conferences and various other conferences both in India and abroad. He inspired and challenged people all over the world. Many in India owe their spiritual foundation to Bakht Singh.

As local churches sprang up across India, walls of separation began to break down and new relationships formed. In the beginning most of the participants in these new local churches were from various denominations. Many of them converted through Bakht Singh's ministry. As Dave Hunt wrote,

> The arrival of Bakht Singh turned the churches of Madras upside down. Upset because their members, who were nearly all nominal Christians, were being converted by thousands through his preaching, crowds gathered in the open air, as many as twelve thousand on one occasion, to hear this man of God preach. Many seriously ill were healed when Bakht Singh prayed for them, even deaf and dumb began to hear and speak.[3]

Criticism toward Bakht Singh from denominational leaders heated up. He was called "exclusive," "non-cooperative," "anti-missions," and "sheep stealer." But his actions demonstrated otherwise. For example, in 1956 Dr. Billy Graham invited Bakht Singh to open his Madras Crusade with prayer, which he gladly accepted. He was on the platform not only with Graham but also with the bishop of Madras and other denomination leaders.

Besides Dr. Billy Graham, he was also acquainted and associated with many evangelical contemporaries from around the world, namely the Reverend John Stott, Dr. Martin Lloyd Jones, Dr. Francis Schaefer, Dr. Norman Grubb, Dr. Christy Wilson, Mr. George Verwer, Dr. Robert Finley, Dr. G.D. James, and others.

G.D. James says of him, "Any other church-planter of this caliber would have let others to have made Bakht Singh a Bishop or Arch Bishop over a thousand large assemblies and hundreds of small churches all over India, Pakistan and Sri Lanka, but he was happy to call himself 'Bakht Singh—the servant of God.' What unswerving dedication! What humility! What a man of God! Was it any wonder that God used his servant so mightily—not only in South Asia but also around the world?"[4]

Notes

1. John Webster Grant, *God's People in India* (Toronto: The Ryerson Press, 1959), pp. 2–3.

2. E. Stanley Jones, *The Christ of the Indian Road* (London: Hodder and Stoughton, 1925), pp. 21–22.

3. Dave Hunt, *God of the Untouchables* (Old Tappan, NJ: Flemming H. Revell Co., 1976).

4. G. D. James, *An Amazing Servant of God*, (See Appendix B).

Part 1

An Apostolic Conversion

Chapter 1

Home-Call

. . . to be absent from the body,
and to be present with the Lord.

2 Corinthians 5:8 KJV

On Friday, September 22, 2000, a large part of the city of Hyderabad, India, came to a standstill. Shops and offices closed. A sea of humanity, perhaps a quarter of a million people, blocked the roads to the cemetery as a procession inched forward with a casket on the top of a van. It took three hours for the procession to reach the cemetery, a distance of three kilometers. Only a fraction of the crowd could get in for the final service. One middle-aged woman from North India said, tears streaming down her face, "All I want is to have a glimpse of his body before it is laid to rest." She expressed the sentiment of tens of thousands who had come from all over India and around the world to pay respects and last tributes to their spiritual father and this godly, gifted leader and servant of Jesus Christ, Bakht Singh of India.

On the previous Sunday, just a few hours before his death, an earthquake shook Hyderabad, coupled with continuous and unusual thunder and lightning. Lights went out and darkness blanketed the area for a while. But on this day, the day of his funeral, just as his casket was being carried out, the sun shone brightly and a rainbow circled it for a short time. After the rainbow disappeared, a shining ring like a crown appeared around the sun. Both the earthquake and the rainbow were reported with pictures in the local daily newspaper. People wondered what these natural phenomena meant. Perhaps Bakht Singh was receiving his crown as he was greeted by Jesus, his Lord and Savior.

He had been sick and bedridden for more that a decade with Parkinson's disease, which took a heavy toll on his health and memory. Since he had been out of touch with most people and places for several years, we, his friends and supporters, did not expect a large crowd at his funeral. We were wrong.

The news of Bakht Singh's home-call spread like wildfire across India and around the world. Thousands traveled to Hebron, the headquarters of his national and international work. Hebron turned into a heaven-like city: people from various backgrounds and fellowship came together to share testimonies, pray, and sing songs of praise and worship continually for twenty-four hours a day for four days. Letters of condolences and sympathy poured in from people of all walks of life. Even some of the political leaders who were opposed to Christianity came to pay respect to Bakht Singh.

Why such an outpouring of love, tears, and honor for this simple man of God who began his ministry as an unknown itinerant preacher about seventy years before in Colonial India? By nature he was an introvert. All of his life he did not want to draw any attention to himself. In the early days, he allowed no one to take his photo or to print any publicity about him or the Lord's work through him: he was determined that nothing should rob God of His glory. To make sure that Christ was given the central place and all the praise, he refused to be introduced at public meetings or allow his name to be announced in the Assemblies or Holy Convocations.

During his ministry Bakht Singh lived simply, with only the basic necessities of life. He owned nothing except his Bible and the clothes on his back, most of which were given to him by others. After he came to know the Lord, he never had a bank account or possessed any worldly goods. He owned neither a car nor a bicycle. He lived in a small room furnished with a simple bed.

When he returned to India following his studies in England and Canada, Bakht Singh's well-to-do parents would have lavished all the comforts, luxuries, and love possible on him, their eldest son. Their only requests were that he return home with them to Karachi and that he be quiet about his commitment to Jesus Christ for the sake of the family prestige. Bakht Singh refused to do so, but instead, to show them respect according to the Indian custom, he gave them all the money he had.

He did not choose nor follow any particular lifestyle as Mahatma Gandhi did, who traveled only third class. Bakht Singh, as the occasion warranted, would travel third class or first class, on foot, or even by bullock-drawn cart. He was naturally at ease with the simple and poor and could closely identify with them, but he was equally relaxed and at ease with the rich and noble. He often stayed with Lady Ogle from London in her lovely bungalow in the Nilgiri Hills. But he stayed just as often in a poor man's hut.

One high-ranking official in the Indian government who attended the funeral said that, in many respects, the honor Bakht Singh received from the hearts of sincere people was much greater and more moving than he had seen at the funeral services of India's foremost political leaders such as Mahatma Gandhi or Pandit Nehru, the first Prime Minister of India.

Why had the Lord honored Bakht Singh so greatly? There are many reasons that stand out. He was willing to leave his comfort zone. When the Lord first called him to ministry in 1930, Bakht Singh told God that he would give all his salary to support the Lord's work but asked God not to make him a preacher. After two years, he finally yielded to the call. Years later while preaching on the subject of "Full Surrender and Service of the Lord," Bakht Singh broke down, recalling that once he had resisted the pleadings of the Holy Spirit for two whole years. As the grief of that old memory flooded his soul, he cried out in self-reproach for his hardness of heart. Suddenly, emotion overcame him, and kneeling down on the platform, publicly he sobbed aloud his gratitude to the Lord for His longsuffering and infinite patience and love. Responsive sobs broke out throughout the large tent until there was scarcely a dry eye in the congregation, strong men as well as women, the aged as well as the young.

Bakht Singh's life's goal was to glorify God in everything, therefore he prayed and sought God's will before doing anything, whether big or small. He lived his life by the threefold conditions that the Lord gave him when He called him to ministry: to tell no man, only the Lord, about his material or financial needs and to withdraw all claims on his father's property in the Punjab; to never join any society but serve all people equally wherever the Lord sent him; and to make no plans of his own but let the Lord lead him day by day. His life's motto was to seek, know, and do the perfect will of God.

Bakht Singh wanted to please God—above his parents, friends, or himself. He wanted to be a true disciple of the Lord and follow in the footsteps of his Master. From his conversion to his home-call, about seventy years, Bakht Singh demonstrated that he loved his Lord more than his parents, wife, child, grandchildren, and even his own life. As a true disciple, he gave up all that he had for Christ—his profession as an engineer, his position as a caste Hindu or Sikh, all his possessions, his inheritance, and his prestige.

From dawn to dusk and many times into the night, Bakht Singh was available to do the service of the Lord. He did not care for his own needs. He walked long distances and slept under trees; he drank from brooks and ate wild fruit without complaint. He was not afraid of anything or anyone when it came to serving the Lord.

Bakht Singh was a man of vision. From the time the Lord gave him a vision of Himself and the church, he remained committed to that vision, planting local churches all across India. He never wavered off course. Talking about Bakht Singh, George Verwer of Operation Mobilization said in 1991, "Bakht Singh has run the race to the very end. I think that is one of the most beautiful things about Bakht Singh, he has run the race to the very end."[1] At no time, even during those long years when his once robust body slowly wasted away and his roaring, lion-like voice was finally silenced, was he ever heard to grumble. He continued his earthly pilgrimage with joy to the end.

Though he was not a great orator or eloquent speaker, the Lord accomplished a great deal through him because he relied totally upon the grace of God. When speaking, he stuttered and stammered.

On one occasion, I asked him why the Lord had used him to heal so many people physically from all kinds of ailments but had not healed him of his speech impediment. He replied that because of the impediment he had to depend upon God whenever he stood to preach or teach. God used him in spite of his limitation.

Bakht Singh was a spiritual father to tens of thousands in Asia as well as a spiritual role model and inspiration to believers around the world. He was India's foremost evangelist, revivalist, and indigenous church-planter. Launching a New Testament church-planting movement that eventually saw hundreds of local churches form throughout India, Pakistan, and parts of Sri Lanka, Bakht Singh could rightly be called the father of indigenous church movement in post-independent India. God used him to spiritually impact his generation both in his homeland and abroad.

Being human, he too had flaws and frailties, but his spiritual strength far outweighed his human weaknesses. His life and ministry are a challenge and inspiration to the church worldwide. The following chapters tell the story of Bakht Singh and the way God used this man whose life was wholly committed to God and His purposes.

Notes
1. Author's interview with George Verwer in 1991 in London.

Chapter 2

Punjabi Childhood

But when God, who set me apart from birth and called me by his grace, was pleased to reveal his Son in me. . . .

Galatians 1:15

Bakht Singh's paternal ancestors were devout Hindus. They also were devotees of Guru Nanak, the founder of Sikhism.[1] Five generations before Bakht Singh's birth, one of his ancestors had no sons. Being a devotee of Guru Nanak, this ancestor prayed that if he were blessed with a son he would make the eldest son a Sikh. His prayers were answered, and the family began the tradition of making the eldest son a Sikh.

For generations, Bakht Singh's family lived in the tiny village of Joiya in the state of Punjab, now part of Pakistan. It had been the home for Bakht Singh's great grandfather Lala Ishwar Das, and now his father, Lala Jawahar Mall.

Jawahar Mall, a successful contractor, built irrigation canals. He was well known and respected for his affluence and position in the village. He and his wife, Srimathi Laxmi Bai, were the wealthiest couple not only in the village of Joiya but also in the surrounding area; their house, a two-story mansion, was the largest in all the thirty-five neighboring villages.

Although greatly blessed materially and respected socially, they were saddened because, after almost eleven years of marriage, they still had no children. It is considered a curse in Indian tradition to have no children, particularly a male child, so the couple offered many prayers, going on pilgrimages from temple to temple. Though a Hindu, Srimathi Laxmi Bai had real faith in Guru Nanak. She prayed often that if she were blessed with a male child, that child would be brought up a Sikh. When she finally conceived, the whole family was excited, hoping the child would be a boy. Instead a daughter was born.

Even though they were blessed with a child, they were not happy. Daughters are not appreciated in India, so prayers and pilgrimages continued for a male child. Laxmi Bai again made her vow to the gods and deities, including Guru Nanak. Before Laxmi Bai conceived a second time, a Sadhu, an Indian holy man, told her she would have a son, but he would not live with her. She pondered over his prediction. Then on June 6, 1903, Laxmi Bai gave birth to a baby boy. In keeping with the family tradition of five generations, Jawahar Mall and Laxmi Bai dedicated their firstborn son to Guru Nanak, vowed to bring him up as a Sikh, and named him Bakht Singh.

Everyone in the village and the neighboring villages knew about the birth of the child. The whole village celebrated with fireworks and singing and dancing in the streets. Several prayers of thanksgiving were offered in the temples.

As Bakht Singh grew up, his parents remembered the words of the Sadhu and feared that perhaps someday Bakht Singh might run away from home to become a Sadhu, so they constantly watched over him and gave him everything he asked for. They never told him no, afraid they might offend him and he would run away from home.

Growing up, Bakht Singh would not play in the streets with other children but would go instead to the temples to find peace. According to Sikh teaching, unless one finds the Satguru, or true teacher, one cannot find peace. So as a child he would ask his mother, "Who is Satguru? How can I find him? Where can I find him?" These questions constantly bothered his young mind. His mother tried to help by telling him that one of the Sadhus can be accepted as Satguru. But this did not satisfy him. "How can they be my Satguru and help me?" he would ask her. This longing of his heart drove him to search for the true and living God. He would spend hours reading Granth Sahib, the holy book of Sikhs.

Bakht Singh's parents planned a lavish celebration for his twelfth birthday. To show off his wealth, popularity, and his love for his son, Jawahar invited people from his village and all the surrounding villages. He even brought in ice for the party. In those days child marriages were practiced in India. So as part of the birthday celebration, Bakht Singh was married to fifteen-year-old Rambai.[2] The joyous celebration lasted for several days.

In 1919, robbers broke into Jawahar's house. They almost killed Jawahar, attacking him with an axe. Fearing that her husband might be killed, Laxmi Bai found the key to the cupboard containing their gold and valuables and threw it to the robbers. They grabbed everything, gold, money, and other valuables, and disappeared into the night, leaving Jawahar bleeding. Realizing that Joiya was no longer a safe place for them to live, the family moved to Sargodha. Over time the family grew as seven more children followed the birth of Bakht Singh.

Young Bakht Singh still yearned to know God. "I think God's hand was upon me from my birth. That gave me a longing to know God. . . . I was not fond of playing at all. I can still picture a very small village, Joiya by name, where I was born. In the village there was a small temple, a small mud house which could seat about twenty people. On the left side there was a small well with a verandah in front. I can still remember that I would sit in one corner when I went there, and say like this, "Sadhu, Satguru, how to find him: where is he?"[3]

Even as a Sikh, he remembers crying like a child, "Oh God, where art Thou? Tell me how to find Thee. And every time I prayed, God seemed so very, very far away; and it seemed that it would take many re-births to get even a glimpse of Him—He was so far away."[4] This childhood yearning to know the true and living God was so strong that he often had disturbing dreams, which were fulfilled later on when he found Christ.

About one of his dreams, he wrote:

> During my school days I used to have a dream. The dream was that I was climbing a high and steep hill. With great difficulty and struggle I would reach the top. As soon as I reached it, somebody would come along and hurl me down. As I fell, the sharp points of the rocks would dig into my ribs. Thus I would be in great pain,

so much so that I would cry out in my dream. But in the end I would find myself lying on soft silk cushions, so soft that I would sink into them. This lying on soft cushions would give me a heavenly feeling, and I would say that if one could get such joy on silk cushions, it was worth undergoing all the pain endured while falling down. When I was at the age of nine or ten I used to have this dream, but about six years ago this dream came to me again and the Voice said to me, "This is your testimony."[5]

Bakht Singh's allegiance to Sikhism made him bitter against the gospel of Christ. Although he was educated in a mission school in the Punjab for seven years, he did not want to know anything about Christ. Most of the boys studying in the school hated Christians and made fun of the Bible teachers and pastors. Hindus and Muslims lived on one side of the boarding house and the Christians on the other. Not once during his stay did he visit the Christian side. Most of the Hindu boys had a similar hatred for Muslims, but they played and talked freely with them; they never made friends with the Christian boys.

Most non-Christians in India viewed Christianity as a religion of the Western white man or thought it was only for the poor and untouchables or outcastes. In the early days missionaries worked among the poor and outcastes who often embraced Christianity for material gain. During the famine in 1905, there was a mass conversion among the untouchables and sweeper class. They became known as "rice Christians." Few of the converts were from caste Hindus and the elite of society. In most cases it was a conversion of convenience, for social uplift and economic advancement rather than of commitment to Christ. As a result the Protestant church in the Punjab grew from about four thousand in 1881 to over forty-eight hundred thousand in 1947. This trend was true all over India.[6]

Well-to-do caste Hindus, Sikhs, and other non-Christians looked down on Christianity and would have nothing to do with Christians. Moreover many missionaries, even those in the mission schools, did not share the gospel with others. Bakht Singh said that he never heard the gospel while he was studying in the mission school.

Furthermore, most Indians formed their impressions and opinions of Christianity and of Christ on the basis of the lifestyle of the British who ruled India. Their loose morals, contemptuous treatment of Indians as inferiors, dietary habits, social life, and other factors repulsed high-caste and well-to-do Indians. It was difficult for the Indians to see the difference between British officials who were mostly nominal Christians and the missionaries; for most Indians, there was not much difference. Moreover, many Indians hated British rulers and, for obvious reasons, considered them India's enemies and exploiters. When Bakht Singh was sixteen, an incident took place in Amirtsar, Punjab, that worsened the bitter hatred and anti-Christian attitude toward the British and missionaries.

In 1919, following World War I, the British parliament passed the Rowlatt Act, designed to repress Indian nationalism. To protest the act, Mahatma Gandhi called for a national hartal, or lock out, on April 7, 1919.

Unfortunately, riots erupted, the most serious of which took place in Amirtsar, Punjab, the holy city of the Sikhs. A mob murdered five Europeans, attempted to murder two English missionary ladies, set fire to an Anglican Church and a mission school with pupils and teachers inside, and looted banks, killing three managers. They also attacked the railway station, the telegraph station, and a town hall. When the matter got out of hand, Lieutenant-governor Sir Michael O'dewyer declared a curfew in the city and called for troops to maintain law and order.

That Sunday was a spring-festival day and several thousand villagers from outside Amirtsar had come to celebrate the festival in an open space hemmed in by rows of houses. Just after the gathering began, Brigadier General Reginald Dyer arrived with his soldiers and, without warning, opened fire with machine guns on the defenseless Indians. For ten minutes, while the trapped Indians (mostly Punjabis) screamed for mercy, the soldiers fired some 1650 rounds, killing or wounding about 1500 people. This event inflamed racial hatred between Indians and the British even more and further fueled anti-Christian and anti-missionary feelings.[7] It was a terrible turning point in the history of British-Indian relations.

Growing up in that anti-Christian climate, Bakht Singh hated Christians and the Bible, as did most of his non-Christian contemporaries. Once when he was given a beautifully bound Bible after passing his intermediate examination, he tore out the contents and kept the beautiful leather cover. He was orthodox in his own religion and spent many hours in Sikh temples observing all the religious rites. As Sikhs are well known for their social service, he also took an active part in such work, but that did not give him the real joy and peace he had been searching for.

Bakht Singh planned to study medicine in the government college after high school. The first choice of most parents in India, then and even now, is that their children become doctors. But God had other plans for him. Assured of getting a seat in the medical college, Bakht Singh would help his father in his factory from time to time while he studied. One day he discovered his father was being deceived by agents selling equipment. He writes: "So I sent a telegram to my father telling him that he was being deceived by the agents, and that he would run a very big loss. Then a thought came to me, 'My father is being deceived by crooked agents. Why don't I become an engineer and help him?' So I decided to study engineering in order to help my father in his factory at Sargodha. This meant I had to go to England for my engineering course."[8]

There was great prestige in those days for Indian young people to study in England. They wanted to show the British, who ruled the country and considered Indians second-class citizens, they were not inferior to white men in any way; they only lacked the opportunity to prove it. Many Indians thought they were far superior to the British, but only the wealthy could send their children to England for studies. Although his father was reluctant to send him, Bakht Singh finally persuaded him, with the help of his mother.

Notes

1. Sikhism: The Sikhs are from the Pujab and originated in a movement of religious reform. Its founder, Guru Nanak, was a contemporary of Martin Luther. The word Sikh means a disciple. The Sikhs wear a distinctive dress and have their own social customs. They accept the Hindu ideas of samsara and karma, and they view themselves as the Khalsa, a chosen race of soldier-saints committed to a Spartan code of conduct and a crusade for righteousness. Hindu families may dedicate one of their children to the Sikh religion.

2. In 1924 when Bakht Singh was 21, he and his wife had a son, Onkar Singh.

3. Author's interview with Brother Bakht Singh, 1978.

4. Bakht Singh, *Return of God's Glory*, (Bombay, India: Gospel Literature Service, 1969), p. 57.

5. Bakht Singh, *How I Got Joy Unspeakable and Full of Glory* (Hyderabad, India: Hebron, 1936), p. 2.

6. Susan Billington Harper, *In the Shadow of the Mahatma* (Grand Rapids, MI: Wm. B. Eerdmans Publishing Company, 2000), pp. 180–181.

7. John Keay, *India, A History*, (New York: Grove Press, 2000), pp. 475–477.

8. Brother Bakht Singh, *Looking Unto Jesus* (Secunderabad, India: B.B.C. Printers & Publishers, 1971, pp. 44–45.

Chapter 3

Education, Experience, and Conversion

*I will instruct you and teach you in the way you should
go; I will counsel you and watch over you.*

Psalm 32:8

When he was seven years old, Bakht Singh's father, a successful
contractor, took him to work and introduced him to the supervising English engineer. The Englishman said, "Why don't you send
your son to England?" Jawahar Mall laughed, "He is too small and
cannot even blow his nose."

"My wife and I will look after him in England," the engineer
told him and then said, "When he returns from England, he will
pull down the stronghold of Brahmanism."[1] Jawahar Mall laughed,
thinking he was joking. The words, "he must go to England" stuck
in Bakht Singh's mind, and he told everyone he would go to England

one day. After graduating, twenty-three-year-old Bakht Singh persuaded his father to let him go. He wanted to go to England to
fulfill his dream, but God had different plans for him, plans that he
would find out about later.

Bakht Singh wrote:

> My ambition in life had been to go to England, travel
> around the world, obtain high education, enjoy the
> friendship of all kinds of people and remain faithful
> to my religion. Similarly, I had a desire to wear smart
> clothes and eat high-class food. . . . I was able to satisfy
> them all.[2]

He made all preparations for travel to England within one
week. Before boarding the ship in Bombay, Bakht Singh had to
obtain his passport in Lahore. The clerk in the secretariat's office
laughed when he told her his trip was in four days. "You will need
at least one month for a passport. If you want one sooner, you
will have to go Simla to see the secretary at the summer capital of
India." Because the journey was six hours by train, Bakht Singh
decided to take a taxi and save four hours. However, the trip to
Simla by taxi was costly, so he looked around for someone to share
it. He found an elderly, heavyset man and his son who were going
to Simla and would share the taxi with him.

At the Home Secretary's office, an official told him. "Young
man, it will take two weeks to get your passport. You must have
a Certified Investigation Department official certify you." Bakht
Singh felt sad as he left the Home Secretary's office. The elderly
gentleman who had shared the taxi with him saw him and asked,
"Why are you so sad?" Bakht Sing told him that he needed a CID
certificate. "I know a young man who is a CID official because I am

a retired collector. I will witness for you with him." So Bakht Singh got his passport within half an hour instead of one month.

Bakht Singh's friend advised him to come prepared to spend three hundred rupees a month in England, but Bakht Singh found he could live comfortably on only eighty rupees a month.[3] Before Bakht Singh could write to his father to tell him not to send him more than 80 rupees a month, his friend said, "Don't be hasty. Wait for a few months and you will learn all about it." Bakht Singh took his friend's advice and sent false accounts to his father such as "I have spent 295.56 rupees this month" even though he had spent only eighty rupees. For seven months, he saved the rest and accumulated 1,600 rupees in his bank account.

For the first few months in England, Bakht Singh remained faithful to his religion. He kept his hair and beard long because Sikhs never shave or cut hair from any part of their body. Even when he wanted to cut his hair and beard, he was afraid of what his friends would think. It took him six months to get up the courage to do it.

Clean-shaven, he said, "I have become an atheist, a socialist, and a free thinker, and I could soon become a full-fledged European." As a Sikh he had never touched tobacco, but he began to smoke expensive cigarettes and bought a gold cigarette case, which he took great pride in showing to everyone. He began drinking liquor and bought expensive clothes. He spent four hundred rupees for a suit and bought expensive shirts, ties, and shoes. In just one month, his seven months of saving were gone. He then realized why his friend had told him to not be hasty.

Bakht Singh later recalled, "With great difficulty, I learned Western customs and manners." Although he never relished Western food, he did learn to eat with a knife and fork. He attended theaters, cinemas, and dance halls. For two years he lived as the Europeans, mastering everything about them. Traveling throughout Europe and England, he visited museums, art galleries, and movies; he wore expensive clothes and ate grand meals. Bakht Singh made friends with both the rich and the poor. He attended social functions and all kinds of amusements and acquired as much education as he wanted. Sill he was not happy. He began to ask his English friends and others if they were happy. He asked students, professors, and clerks. Yet he did not find anyone who was really happy.

Before coming to England, Bakht Singh thought that education and sanitation would remove all evils from India. Now he saw that England could not get rid of her evils by education and sanitation but, rather, was full of far more evil than India. He became convinced that culture and education could not solve human problems. He expressed it this way: "a poor man in India uses a dirty rag to cover his wound, while a rich man in England conceals his wound with a beautiful, white bandage three yards long, neither of which, however, can remove the pus and the dirt underneath."

Bakht Singh never encountered a committed Christian who spoke to him directly about Christ. He played tennis at his club every Sunday morning. Later in the day, he would hear Mrs. Kemp, his landlady, playing hymns on the piano. He had no idea what hymns were since he had never gone to a church service. She would invite him into her parlor and play for him. "Do you like this kind of music?" she asked him.

"Yes, Madam, very nice," he would say to be polite, but he really liked popular music, jazz, and Mozart. "I believe that even though she never spoke to me about salvation she must have been praying for me," Bakht Singh said later. She was very kind to him, did his laundry, washed his socks, and did all kinds of jobs for him.

Early one February morning at his college in South Kensington, London, he noticed a large poster with a big question mark and these words, "Why not spend your summer vacation in Canada?" The word Canada attracted him. Upon enquiry, he discovered that a party of twenty-five university students was going to Canada to take part in harvesting crops. The plan was to work on the farms for six weeks during harvest to earn money and then go sightseeing for the remaining six weeks. Even though he was warned that Asians were not welcomed in all parts of Canada, he signed up for the trip. Little did he know that this trip would change his life forever.

The party left Liverpool for Montreal in August of 1928. To prove that he was in no way inferior to any Westerner, Bakht Singh participated in all kinds of activities such as games, drinking, card playing, smoking, and dancing. He even attended a church service held on Sunday morning, afraid that if he did not attend, his friends would think he was a narrow-minded Indian.

Bakht Singh had no interest in the Bible, but to show that he could do what all his companions did, he went to the service and sat in the last row. While the preacher preached, Bakht Singh slept. Towards the end of the service the congregation knelt down to pray. Bakht Singh was the only one still sitting on a chair. He thought to himself, "These people do not know anything about my religion. They have exploited my country. I have seen them eating and drinking, what do they know? After all, my religion is the best religion." His national, intellectual, and religious pride prevented him from kneeling down. He tried to walk out but was hemmed in on both sides by kneeling people.

Then he thought, "I have been to Muslim mosques and Hindu temples. I have taken off my shoes and washed my feet to show my respect for those places. I must honor this place out of courtesy." So to be polite, he overcame his pride and knelt down. He later wrote about what happened next:

> The very moment I knelt down, I felt that some divine power had engulfed me, and I uttered these words, "Lord Jesus, I know and I believe Thou art the living Christ." I kept on repeating the same words again and again. Indeed, I had been an atheist till then, and in my folly I had often said there was no God. From that day, the words "living Christ" somehow became very real to me. This experience left me with a strong desire to know more of the living Lord Jesus. Until then I had absolutely no idea of either the life or the teaching of the Lord Jesus Christ.[4]

The first change Bakht Singh noticed was the great joy that flooded into his soul. And he kept repeating "Lord Jesus," that name he had once despise and made fun of. His attitude toward the English changed. Bakht Singh had felt superior to them, saying that he belonged to an ancient country with an ancient culture. Now he felt that all were equal, Indian and English.

He went back to Canada for a second time, this time to finish his training in agricultural engineering. He met Owel Hansen, a bank manager. Mr. Hansen was different from the other people Bakht Singh met; he seemed happy; his face was always shining. Bakht Singh longed to know what made Hansen happy, so he asked him. This is the same question he had been asking for years to different people, professors, friends, and students. Hansen replied that his happiest experience was when he received the Lord Jesus Christ as his personal savior. Bakht Singh asked Hansen for a New Testament. Hansen was surprised a Hindu and an Indian would want to read the Bible. "You are right. These very hands have torn up a Bible. These very lips have blasphemed against Christ. But for the last eighteen months I have had a great love for the Lord Jesus. I love His name, which sounds so sweet to me. But I do not know yet anything about His life and teaching."[5]

That same night Bakht Singh started reading from the first chapter of the first gospel. He kept on reading until three o'clock in the morning. When he woke up he found the ground covered with snow, so he remained in his room all day reading. He read continuously for three days and became fully convinced that no man could write such a book. Believing that it was God's book, Bakht Singh had read it through with reverence.

On the third day, December 16, 1929, he was reading St. John's gospel when he came to the third chapter, third verse and could go no further. The words "Verily, verily I say unto you" convicted him. As he read these words, his heart began to beat faster. He felt as though someone were standing by his side, saying the same words to him again and again. He had always thought that the Bible belonged to Europeans and Americans, and Indians had their own holy books. When he heard that voice he realize the Bible belonged to him too. He knelt down and said, "Lord, I am a great sinner. I've torn up the Bible and spoken words of blasphemy against Thee and Thy Word, and I have been living a life of shame for many years. Is there any hope for a man like me?"

He looked down and found his body covered with black spots that gave off a bad odor. The voice came again saying, "Bakht Singh, this bad smell and the black spots are because of your sins."

Bakht Singh admitted, "It is quite true. I have committed sins. I have money but no peace; I have education, but my life is a failure."[6]

All of the sins of his school and college days came before him. He felt like the greatest sinner, with a wicked and filthy heart. He saw his petty jealousies against his friends and enemies. He knew his parents thought he was a good boy, and his friends considered him a good friend and a decent member of society, but only he knew his real condition. With tears rolling down his cheeks, Bakht Singh cried, "Oh Lord, forgive me. Truly I am a great sinner. There is no hope for me, a great sinner."

As he was crying the voice said, "This is my body broken for you; this is my blood shed for the remission of your sins. Go, thy sins are forgiven thee." He did not know how but he believed that only the blood of Jesus could save him, and he had the assurance that all his sins were washed away. He felt joy, and peace flood his soul.

For Christmas a few days later, Mr. Hansen gave him a whole Bible. Bakht Singh started with the book of Genesis and read for fourteen hours at a stretch. He finished reading the entire Bible in two months and read the New Testament several times. He started over and read the Bible a second and a third time and gave up reading anything else. He writes about how he began his walk with God:

> I began to read the book of Genesis in the month of January 1930. I found these words again and again in the same chapter: "God said," "God said." I found these words repeated 500 hundred times, and this fragment was a blessing to me: "God speaks, God speaks." So I said, "Oh, God, speak to me. I want to hear Thy voice. I have no ambition for any other experience. The longing of my soul is for You to speak to me." I believed like a

child. Even though it may take some time to learn the lesson that God must speak, the fact remains that when He becomes real, He does speak. A day came when I began to hear His voice every day.[7]

Notes

1. Hindu society is divided into four main castes—*Brahmin, Vaishya, Kshathria, and Shudra.* Beyond these are those technically outside the caste system all together. They are called untouchables or scheduled castes.

   Brahmins have maintained their status practically unchanged throughout the centuries. They are the original priests, religious leaders, and philosophers. Because of their position, they still exert extensive influence in society throughout India. A few Indian prime ministers, including the first Prime Minister, the late Jawaharlal Nehru, were Brahmins.

2. Bakht Singh, *How I Got Joy Unspeakable and Full of Glory* (Bombay, India: Gospel Literature Service, 1936), p. 3.

3. In 1925, 5,537 Rupees were equal to one British Pound. Now about 75 rupees are equal to one British Pound.

4. Bakht Sing, *Hebron Messenger* editorial, August 18, 1968.

5. Bakht Singh, *How I got Joy Unspeakable and Full of Glory*, p. 10.

6. Bakht Singh, *Hebron Messenger*, August 25, 1974, no. 17.

7. Bakht Singh, *The Voice of the Lord* (Bombay, India: Gospel Literature Service, 1970), p. 19.

Chapter 4

A Chosen Vessel

*But the Lord said unto him, Go thy way: for he is
a chosen vessel unto me, to bear my name before the
Gentiles, and kings, and the children of Israel.*

Acts 9:15 KJV

Poverty

The year following the stock market crash in 1929 was the hardest year of depression for all of North America. Thousands were left unemployed. Formerly wealthy people went from house to house selling biscuits and cakes to earn their living. Long soup lines formed in front of soup kitchens, with people standing for hours to get something to eat. At this same time, the newly converted Bakht Singh found himself stranded in Winnipeg, Canada. Many months had passed since he had heard from his parents. Even though he wrote letters and sent cables, he had no news from home. Before his conversion his father had sent him money regularly for whatever he needed. Now he was out of money and had no money left to contact them. He found out later that all of their money was tied up in a legal court case in the Punjab High Court.

Living in a strange city, Bakht Singh did not have a single friend but was determined he would never ask any man for help. He decided to look for a job to support himself. He got up early every morning and walked from place to place—workshops, factories, and shops—asking for a job. The answer was always the same: "I have no job for you. I am very sorry; there is nothing for you." He did this every day for several months.

Then he met some people who invited him to their home because they wanted to taste real Indian curry. It was a friendly gathering; Bakht Singh prepared an Indian curry for two or three people. They liked it and told him that if he were willing to work as a cook, they would help him find a job, even though he was not a cook by profession. This was his first job, and he thanked God for it. As he worked, cutting up onions and peppers and making the sauce, God was teaching him. The Word of God was becoming very real to him.

God, watching over him, sent help through Mr. Hansen who had given him the Bible after his conversion. Mr. Hansen was a tenant in John and Edith Hayward's home and introduced Bakht Singh to them. When Mr. Hansen was hospitalized with a serious illness, he asked the Haywards to let Bakht Singh use his room. Bakht Singh stayed with the Haywards for about three years until he left Vancouver for India in 1933. The Haywards, members of a

Christian Missionary Alliance Church, treated Bakht Singh as part of their family, and their home became a place of training for him.

Before the Haywards were married, Edith had wanted to go to India as a missionary, but she could not go. Instead the Lord sent Bakht Singh to them so that they might disciple him for work in India and around the world. Little did they realize when they took in a newly converted international student that he would one day be the greatest evangelist and church-planter in India in the twentieth century.

While lying on his bed one morning a few months after his conversion, Bakht Singh suddenly saw a map of India on the wall before him, with a shining cross in the center. He heard a voice saying, "If you want to serve me, you have to lay down your life at the cross." At the time he did not understand it or how he could ever serve the Lord, but that bright cross always reminded him that one day he would have to go to India with God's message.

Mr. and Mrs. Hayward opened their home to many visitors, particularly missionaries. They had a son and a daughter, eleven and thirteen years old respectively. Bakht Singh learned the secret of prevailing prayer through the children who prayed for the needs of the missionaries in various parts of the world.

Living with the Haywards, Bakht Singh learned valuable lessons through their lives as well as studied the Bible with them. As Mr. Hayward put it, "Bakht Singh would sit and read the Bible for hours. When something came up in the Bible, he would run down to Edith and ask her many questions. Then he would argue about the Bible and never give in. We had many discussions, and many times it came out as an argument. One day Edith told him that he should not read the Bible any more but get down on his knees and ask God to reveal himself to him, and open the Scriptures so that the Holy Spirit could teach him."

Laxmi Bai, Bakht Singh's mother, sent a letter to Edith Hayward to thank the Haywards for taking care of her son. She wrote that she had made several pilgrimages and visited many shrines in India so that she might bear a son, and now that son was stranded in a far off country. Unable to support him financially due to their own financial problems, she suggested that the Haywards consider him as their own son. They became like parents to him and made him a home away from home. He even called them "Dad" and "Mom."

Growing in the Lord

While reading the Scriptures, Bakht Singh came to Hebrews 13:8: "Jesus Christ the same yesterday, today, and forever." Sinus congestion had bothered him for many years, and he had consulted the best English doctors, but they were unable to help him. His eyesight, too, was weak. Reading that Jesus Christ was the same yesterday, today, and forever gave him the confidence to pray, "Will you heal my nose and give me good sight?" The next morning he found that he had been healed. From then on he prayed for the healing of many, and the Lord answered his prayers.

Bakht Singh spent hours in the library reading the Scriptures and other Christian books. As he grew in the Lord, he began teaching the Haywards rather than they always teaching him. "In a few months after his conversion, he was ready to face the world and preach the gospel," said John Hayward. "Some missionaries wanted to sponsor him, but he preferred to be independent. We often tried to get him sponsored through Christian and Missionary Alliance church (CMA), but he did not want to do it."

When the Haywards moved from Winnipeg to Vancouver, Bakht Singh moved with them. They attended West Broadway Baptist Church, and on February 4, 1932, Bakht Singh was baptized—more than two years after his conversion. He explained why it took him more than two years to decide to be baptized:

> For two years, after my conversion, I never thought of baptism. I read the Bible every day. Sometimes I used to spend a whole day with the Bible, but was not baptized, thinking that it was not necessary. One Saturday morning . . . the Lord spoke to me through Matthew 3:13. "Then cometh Jesus from Galilee to Jordan unto John, to be baptized of him." (KJV) The Lord said to me clearly, "Are you in any way better than your Savior?" I replied, "Lord, I never said so." He said, "Then what about baptism?" I had been thinking that baptism was not very important because I was born again and giving my testimony everywhere . . . I was baptized the very next day. . . . I was filled with great joy when I came out of the water. From that day onwards, the Bible became a new book to me. I enjoyed much liberty in prayer and witnessing. Everything became new to me.[1]

One morning Bakht Singh received a telephone call enquiring whether he would be able to speak on a certain Sunday. After checking his diary, he told the enquirer that he was free and would be glad to accept. The Haywards overheard this conversation and asked him, "Don't you pray and find God's perfect will before accepting any invitation to go out and speak?" He replied, "There is no need to find God's perfect will for this matter. I am not going for my personal work but to give God's message." He was offended and thought they were finding fault with him. So much so that he did not speak to them or even say "Good morning" to them for two weeks.

But the more Bakht Singh thought about it, he realized he did not know how to find God's will. He decided not to accept any invitation to speak or even visit anyone until he learned how to be sure about the Lord's will. He often went to the seaside by himself to pray the whole day, asking the Lord to teach him how to find His will.

Pushed into Ministry

Bakht Singh was a reluctant evangelist and preacher, without the slightest desire to become one. One time shortly after his conversion, he attended a small meeting of Christians. A man asked him where he was from, and Bakht Singh told him he was from India. At the end of the meeting, the man announced to the group that someone from India was going to speak to them. Bakht Singh looked around the room; he was glad to find another Indian there. Little did he know, however, that he was the one from India. The man took him to the front of the group and introduced him. Bakht Singh was quite shy and had never preached before. He looked down and muttered something softly. He told them he was a sinner and the Lord had saved him. He did not think anyone heard him, and after speaking, he ran out. He became angry and promised himself that he would never go back there again. One of the men on the same platform with him ran out after him. "God bless you," he said. "Your testimony was of great blessing to me." This man later became Bakht Singh's best friend. The thought then came to Bakht Singh that maybe the Lord was able to use even the weakest creature.

Another time a man asked him to please come to their church and speak to them next Sunday. Bakht Singh told him that he was not a preacher, but the man said, "We want a man from India to speak." Bakht Singh reluctantly agreed. He went, not knowing what he would say. As he stood to speak, he began to tremble. He looked up and prayed, "Lord, have mercy upon me and touch my lips and enable me to speak." The words came slowly; he stuttered and stammered at first, but then began to speak loudly. A man ran up to him afterwards and said, "The Lord sent you to comfort me." Bakht Singh did not know how the words came to him that day. He had not read any books nor done any public speaking, and he was very shy.

Bakht Singh was literally pushed into ministry. Many people began to invite him to speak, but he tried to refuse. He thought he had no qualifications to become a preacher, and since he could not sing one note, he said to himself, "A man who cannot sing, can he preach? A man who stutters, can he preach?" For one full year he was pushed, never knowing what he would say when he began to preach. At the beginning of each meeting, he called upon the Lord, and the Lord continued to help him.

Toronto

A firm in Toronto, about 2000 miles east of Winnipeg, offered him training in agricultural engineering in their factory and, later, a job. He did not have money, however, to buy the ticket for the trip to Toronto. He knelt down and prayed, "Lord, if you want me to go there, please provide me with the railway fare." After the Sunday service the next day, a man asked Bakht Singh to go to Toronto for him. He was the police superintendent in Toronto and needed two policemen to travel by special train from Winnipeg to Toronto.

Bakht Singh became a policeman for two days—God's provision for his fare.

Bakht Singh had very little money in Toronto. With his last few cents, he bought a packet of cocoa without sugar. He mixed this cocoa with hot water from the bathroom and drank it each morning, mid-day, evening, and night. This is all he ate for ten days even though he was working long days in the factory and walking many miles to and from home—he had no money for bus fare. Looking back, Bakht Singh remembered those were extremely happy days, and he was thankful for all the trials because the Lord became very real to him then.

There were times, however, when Bakht Singh felt miserable and dejected and thought how much better off he had been before his conversion. Then he had money in two banks and could even lend money to friends. Now he had no money to buy food. The weather was very cold, and he did not have warm clothing and had to walk the long distance to and from work. Shivering with cold one day, he saw, in front of a church building, a small board with a fragment from Hebrew 2:18, "He is able to succor them that are tempted." He began to repeat it several times. He could not explain the meaning of the words, yet they were of great help to him, expelling his sorrow. He went into the workshop singing in his heart and repeating those words, "He is able. He is able to succor them that are tempted." Afterwards, even in extreme trouble, those words came to him and brought him much encouragement. Bakht Singh testified, "Like that, we have happy experiences as to how the Lord met us and how he spoke to us, and the comfort and inspiration which we receive from God's Word, we cannot receive from any man. This is the experience that I cannot forget."

Then came the winter. In Canada the winter is extremely cold, and unless one has extra-warm clothing, it is very difficult to keep warm. Bakht Singh prayed every morning and night that the Lord would keep him warm, as he had no money to buy a sweater, a muffler, a scarf, or an overcoat. He drew his knees up to his chest at night to keep himself warm. But the Lord began to speak to him in the early hours. Bakht Singh knew that God had a hidden plan was allowing these hardships to come into his life.

He walked many miles in shoes with holes in the soles. One day Bakht Singh asked God to give him a new pair of shoes; he was determined not to give a hint or suggestion to anyone that he was hungry or needed anything. That day he had an appointment with a gentleman, so he polished up his old shoes and called at his office. During the conversation, the gentleman suddenly broke off and said, "Would you mind if I buy you a new pair of boots? Please do not say no. Someone has given me money to buy a new pair of boots."

One morning Bakht Singh felt a strong urge to write to his mother, but he had no money to buy stamps or stationary. He knelt down and prayed, "Lord, I believe my mother is thinking about me and I would like to write to her. I have no money to buy stamps and paper." He got up from his knees and felt something in his pocket. It was a small coin. Doubtful that this coin was enough to buy stamps, he called a child, gave him the coin, and sent him to buy the stamps. Presently, a lady came back with the coin and demanded to know why he had given the child such a valuable coin. She said it was a rare gold coin, which she had not seen for many years. Bakht Singh questioned how a gold coin could be in his pocket and thought it must be copper. But she confirmed it was gold, and he was able to send the letter to his mother that day.

Surrender

Realizing his own limitations as a preacher and public speaker, Bakht Singh planned to return to India, make money in the field of agricultural engineering and use his earnings to support the Lord's work in India. After much thought and planning, he came up with a plan for a Christian agricultural model colony called "The Village of the Cross." He wanted to buy a large piece of agricultural land for the government and develop it in the shape of a cross. About this plan Daniel Smith wrote:

> The life of the residents of "The Village of the Cross" was to be a testimony to India of Christian life and love. Other parts of the cross-shaped village were to be divided into sections for the growth of sugar cane, cotton, coarse grain, medicinal herbs, spices, vegetables, fruits, date palms, and mulberry trees. The Lord was to have a tithe of all. Such was the grandiose scheme of Bakht Singh's newly converted mind. But before he could move away from Canada and put his scheme into effect, another great spiritual crisis was to change the whole pattern of his service and move him into the realm of the Lord's own purposes. The call, clear and insistent, was to preaching. . . . This meant that "The Village of the Cross" would be ruled out, since it represented a scheme of his own brain. His own things had to die. Thus it was that his grandiose scheme was carried to its funeral and buried before it ever came into being. From that day on Bakht Singh was to take infinite pains to know the Lord's mind about every small detail of life.[2]

He was invited to speak to a small group of young people. They asked Bakht Singh to tell them about Christian work in India. As he spoke he continuously found fault with the missionaries and their work in India. When he returned to his room that night, he could not pray. Then the Lord said to him very clearly, "Who are you to find fault with My servants? What about you? Why don't you take up the work yourself?" Bakht Singh replied, "Lord, I do not have the least qualification to be a public speaker. That is the reason I have been hesitating to surrender my life to You for Your service; instead I will give You all my money for Your work."

The Lord said to him, "I do not want your money, I want you."

Bakht Singh then said to the Lord, "But since You want me in spite of my many handicaps, I am ready to serve You and go anywhere You send me." That morning he knelt down and asked for forgiveness and said, "Oh Lord, will You accept me? I am prepared to go anywhere whether to India, China, or Africa. I am going to give up everything for You—friends, relatives, and belongings."

The Lord said to him, "You will have to live by faith. You must not ask for anything, not even from your friends or relations. You must not ask even for a cup of coffee."

"Who is going to provide for my needs?" Bakht Singh asked of the Lord. "That is not your business," was the Lord's reply. He marked the day and time on April 4, 1932, at 2:30 AM when he surrendered himself to the Lord. Then he heard the Lord say, "I accept you for My service on three conditions:

> Withdraw all your claims to your father's property in the Punjab and never tell any man about your material and financial needs by letter or by suggestion of any kind. Tell it only to Me.

> Do not join any society, but serve all people equally, wherever I send you.
>
> Do not make your own plans, but let Me lead you day by day.

He replied, "Lord, I agree," and it was settled. His heart was flooded with the love of Christ for all people, and the Lord opened doors for him to go to many places as his witness. Daniel Smith wrote, "Such was the movement of the Spirit in calling Bakht Singh into his grace. . . . 'I felt I loved everybody,' he said, 'My heart flowed out even to the Westerners whom I had long despised.'"[3]

In October of 1932, Bakht Singh wrote to his father about his conversion and then prayed that the Lord might send someone to his father to explain the letter since it was long and had many references to the Bible. His father went to see the American missionary in his hometown and said, " I have a letter from my son containing many references from the Bible. Can you explain them to me?" The missionary gave him a Bible in Urdu and taught him how to look up the references. After looking up all the references, he was convinced that his son's conversion was according to real conviction. He therefore had no objection and wrote to his son that he was pleased to know that he was happy in his faith.

Vancouver is a famous seaport. While living there, he was able to talk to Africans, Japanese, Chinese, Italians, Hungarians, and other nationalities from many countries, sharing the gospel with them. Bakht Singh also visited Indian families and shared the gospel with them. That was how the Lord trained him for service in India.

Bakht Singh prayed and asked for the Lord's plan and direction for his future, and the Lord said to him, "I want you to leave for India on the sixth of February, 1933."[4] Bakht Singh went to the shipping office to enquire if there was ship leaving Vancouver for India on February 6. They took down his name and told him he could pay the fare on the day of sailing. He informed his friends that he was leaving, and they promptly arranged a farewell gathering for two days before his departure. The day before the farewell, Bakht Singh still did not have the money for his passage to India, so the gathering was canceled in spite of the fact that Bakht Singh still believed that he was going to India on the sixth as the Lord had told him. Then, just in time for him to sail, he received more than the amount he needed for the passage, and, as the Lord had revealed, Bakht Singh sailed for Bombay, India on the sixth of February 1933.

Notes

1. Bakht Singh, *The Strong Foundation* (Hyderabad, India: Hebron, 1972), pp. 8–9.
2. Daniel Smith, *Bakht Singh of India, A Prophet of God* (Charlottesville, VA: Christian Aid Mission, 1957), pp. 37–38.
3. Ibid., p. 39.
4. Bakht Singh, *How I Got Joy Unspeakable and Full of Glory* (Bombay, India: Gospel Literature Service, 1939), p. 34.

Chapter 5

Itinerant Preacher: Bombay and Beyond

1933 to 1935

I will instruct you and teach you in the way you should go; I will counsel you and watch over you.

Psalm 32:8

Bombay

When Bakht Singh arrived in Bombay in April of 1933, his parents met him there and welcomed him with tears of joy. But soon their tears of joy turned into tears of pain and agony.

Following the excitement of meeting his son, Jawahar Mall, Bakht Singh's father, took him aside and told him that he had no objection to his becoming a Christian because he was old enough to decide to follow the religion of his choice. However, he had one request: while Bakht Singh was in their hometown of Sargodha, he should keep his faith a secret. To this Bakht Singh replied that the Lord Jesus Christ was his life and he could no more deny the Lord than he could stop breathing. His father was shocked to find out that not only had Bakht Singh become a Christian, but he had also become a full-time preacher and would not keep his faith a secret.

Bakht Singh's father begged him to at least get a job and help support the family. Because of the long court case, previously mentioned, his father had lost most of his wealth. The family had been going through severe financial difficulties, and there were still young brothers and sisters at home. But Bakht Singh told him if one soul were lost through his disobedience to the Lord's call, that soul would be, in his eyes, worth more than losing the whole world. Furthermore, he assured his father that the Lord would take care of the family and would supply the needs of all his brothers and sisters. Later the Lord indeed honored Bakht Singh's faith and heard his prayers on behalf of all his siblings; all five brothers and three sisters were able to complete their studies and find excellent jobs.

Seeing Bakht Singh's unwavering commitment to the Lord and refusal to comply with his request to keep quiet about his faith for even a short time while he stayed with them, his brokenhearted father humbled himself: he took off his turban and placed it at the feet of his son and begged him to change his mind. This act was very humbling for his father, but he was willing to do anything to have his son with him. Conversion to Christianity was considered to be against the family prestige of the well-to-do high-caste Hindus, Sikhs, and other non-Christians in India. Many in India, even today, think that Christianity is essentially a white man's religion, and that only the low-caste and outcastes follow Christianity.

When Jawahar Mall realized that Bakht Singh would not change his mind, he told his son that he could not go home with them even though he had been out of the country for seven years. To show his respect to his father, Bakht Singh gave him all the money he had. Before the sorrow-stricken parents boarded the train at Victoria Terminus in Bombay to return home to Sargodha, his mother pleaded with him again, sobbing, "My son, I offered many prayers and shed tears before you were born. Please, for my sake, can't you keep quiet about your faith at least for a while? Please, please?"

Bakht Singh replied, crying also, "Mother, I love you so dearly, but how can I deny my Lord who gave His life for me?" The words of the Sadhu, who told her before the birth of Bakht Singh that she would be blessed with a son but that he would not stay with her, pierced through her heart.

After the train disappeared from sight, Bakht Singh, wiping tears from his eyes, stood on the platform and asked the Lord for guidance. Rejected by his parents, penniless, homeless, helpless, yet with hope, he remembered words from Psalm 27:10: "When my father and my mother forsake me, then the LORD will take me up" (KJV). Then the words he had heard in Vancouver came to his mind, "Do not make your own plans but let Me lead you day by day. Tell no man about your material or financial needs. Tell them only to Me." That night the Lord led him to a public shelter where he was given a free room for a week.

He began witnessing for Christ in the city of Bombay by distributing gospel tracts. Some who were interested would offer him a cup of tea. Sometimes this would be his only food for the day. He was homeless, foodless, friendless, but joyful. He remembered the words of the apostle Paul, "He that spared not His own Son, but delivered Him up for us all, how shall He not with Him also freely give us all things?" (KJV).

After the week at the public shelter, he asked God for guidance for a place to stay and remembered someone he had met in Scotland in 1928. Mrs. Maclane was a missionary for whom he had prepared a curry dinner while staying at a boarding house in Edinburgh. She had invited him to visit her in Bombay whenever he returned to India. Her husband was a professor at Wilson College in Bombay. Bakht Singh went to the college to pay a courtesy call but was told that the Maclanes had moved back to Scotland. As he was about to leave, the watchman said, "Sir, there is another missionary here whom you can meet." Since he had no good reason not to stay, Bakht Singh went with the man to meet the missionary: Mr. Warner, superintendent of the Methodist Mission in Bombay. Mr. Warner was very glad to meet Bakht Singh, and after hearing his testimony of how Jesus Christ had changed his life, he told Bakht Singh that there was a great need for speakers that weekend because it was Easter weekend and there were special meetings in a number of places all over Bombay. Mr. Warner invited Bakht Singh to stay at the church facility, which was also his own residence and the residence of the bishop of the Methodist churches, Bishop Bradley.

About this contact, Bakht Singh writes:

> During the same time, I met Bishop Bradley, one of the main speakers of Sialkot Convention in West Punjab. . . . Through his influence, I was invited . . . to speak at the Sialkot Convention, which in those days was one of the largest conventions in Punjab. I accepted and that gave me an entrance to almost all parts of Punjab. Even

though I had returned to India with no plan of my own
and did not know where to begin and what to do, . . .
the same person gave me a letter of introduction to a co-
worker in Karachi . . . and from there I had the honor of
taking the gospel to many parts of Sindh, even to remote
villages.[1]

Karachi

While he was living and working in Bombay, Bakht Singh received a letter from his sister inviting him to Karachi. The bishop
put him in touch with some missionaries working in Karachi, one
of whom was an American, Mr. Gray. After visiting his sister, Bakht
Singh went to see Mr. Gray, who sent him to the Indian pastor,
Reverend Shabaz, who lived behind Mr. Gray's compound. Bakht
Singh found Pastor Shabaz down with a fever that day. "Brother,
the Lord has sent you for my sake. Today is Saturday, tomorrow is
Sunday, and I have no one to preach. Will you kindly preach for me
tomorrow?" he asked. That was Bakht Singh's first church meeting
in India, and he was asked to come back again.

Pastor Shabaz told him that there were five thousand nominal Christian Punjabi sweepers with nothing being done for them
because they were all drunkards and gamblers. They had become
Christians during the great famine of 1905, but now no one cared
about them in their life of shame.

So Bakht Singh began working among the sweepers in Karachi.
Most of these people were low-caste Punjabis, living in Muhallas
(slum-like communities). Meetings were held in open spaces beside open sewers. One day some people brought a young man on a
stretcher who wanted to hear the message. He was a college graduate and was suffering from a high fever. After a few days, Bakht

Singh decided to visit the young man with the fever and was saddened to hear the boy had died. He went instead to visit the parents to tell them that he was very sorry to hear their son had passed away. Several had gathered around, sitting with the parents. Bakht Singh opened his Bible and gave a short message. The parents were happy he had come and invited him back. He went every evening, and people came out onto the street to listen. And the Lord began to save souls.

Bakht Singh began Bible study and prayer meetings for the sweepers at four o'clock in the morning because they had to go to work very early to sweep the streets and clean the public toilets. They would kneel by their baskets and brooms and sing Punjabi songs. When they went to work, they sang their sweet songs while they worked, sweeping the streets and roads. They began to compose Punjabi songs. These born-again Punjabi sweepers were inspired. They were simple folks singing simple songs, but they were full of life.

Bakht Singh held preaching meetings in the open air twice a day in different parts of Karachi with the help of those "singing saints." He went wherever they lived and visited them in their homes. Whatever money they collected he gave to Pastor Shabaz.

His sister, when she heard he was preaching in the bazaar and working among the sweepers, wrote to her father saying, "Things are dangerous, please come soon to Karachi." His father came and brought Bakht Singh's wife. Bakht Singh's wife became convinced that he was not going to renounce Christ, and she left him, never to see him again. His son never came to see him either.

The family gathered in his sister's home. His sister, brother-in-law, brothers, and his father became very angry and began to shout at him, saying that he had left a high and noble religion and become an outcaste. Bakht Singh replied, "I am worse than an outcaste because you cannot see the state of my heart. The Lord Jesus has told me that I am the greatest sinner."

His sister became very angry when he said this and spoke against Christ. His father asked for an Urdu Bible and began to read certain passages from the New Testament. The sister said, "We sent for you to reprimand him, but now you are preaching Christ, too."

Their father replied, "You have no right to say anything against the Lord Jesus Christ because you do not know anything about Him. You can say what you want against your brother but do not say anything against Christ."[2]

The next day his father told Bakht Singh the story of how he had searched for peace after they had parted that day at the train station in Bombay. He visited sadhus and sanyasis, Hindu priests, to ask them how to get peace. None of them could tell him. He visited a well near Amritsar in Punjab with eighty-four steps. It was believed that if someone said eight-four prayers—one step and one day at a time for eighty four days, he would attain salvation. He did this but obtained no peace.

He then visited a church, and as he sat in the back, just as the service began, he saw a great light and cried, "Oh Lord, You are my Savior, too." When he said this, great peace filled his soul. He had a huge legal case against his partner who had swindled him, which had been going on for ten years and had cost him a great deal of money, time, and strength. However, when he was born again at the age of seventy-two, he destroyed all the papers saying, "Thank God He made me poor so I could find Christ."

Before leaving Karachi, his father said to him, "You can come home whenever you want." So Bakht Singh went home, and all his friends and relatives came to see him. From morning until night they reproved him with negative comments. Although everyone had something to say, Bakht Singh kept quiet. Then his father asked him to give his testimony in the local church. The church was afraid there would be trouble and it would be dangerous, but Bakht Singh said he was prepared for everything.

Meetings were held in the newly built church, and people of all classes came until there was hardly room, inside or out. After Bakht Singh gave his testimony, many gathered around to ask questions. The first question was, "Does your religion allow you to disobey your parents? When your father has spent so many rupees on your education, surely it was your duty to ask his consent before you became a Christian. Look at you father; he is broken-hearted. Do you call this love?"

Bakht Singh was about to answer but his father spoke up. "I am not broken-hearted at all. Why do you drag my name into it? I am convinced that my son has real peace. Before you ask any more questions, I want to know whether there is anyone here with real peace, eternal peace. I will not allow anyone to ask questions unless he has real peace." With that the crowd began to disperse. After that Bakht Singh visited his hometown of Sargodha many times and conducted several meetings in the local churches. The hatred his family once had against him was gone.

Bakht Singh's Family

Later, in October 1945, Bakht Singh had a dream. He was standing on the bank of a wide river and saw his father standing on the other side. Then he saw his father swimming toward him.

When he got to the other side, he was out of breath, so Bakht Singh pulled him out of the river. When Bakht Singh woke up, he prayed that the Lord would tell him the meaning of the dream.

The Lord said, "The time of your father's departure is near. He is not ready, go to him." So he went to Punjab from Madras and asked his father, "Father, has the Lord spoken to you in any way?"

His father said, "Yes, he has spoken to me to come to Madras and give my testimony and be baptized." He had been avoiding baptism for more than two years. That December he was baptized by Bakht Singh in Madras, along with forty-five other people. He gave his testimony, which was translated into two languages and lasted for three hours. That was one of the happiest days in Bakht Singh's life who, with a beaming face, called his father "brother" as he baptized him.

A great change took place in his father. He came out of the water with a shining face and said; "I never knew that it is so wonderful to obey God like this." The next Sunday, Bakht Singh told him, "You are an old man and cannot sit for the meeting that begins at ten o'clock and ends around four o'clock. It is five or six hours long. You can come only for a while."

His father simply replied, "No, I want my full blessing: I will come at the beginning." He would not even sit on the pillow or take any food or water that Bakht Singh offered him. He sat in front of Bakht Singh for the entire six hours to take part in the whole meeting. He was so happy. A few months after his baptism, Bakht Singh's father was called to glory while Bakht Singh was in Scotland.

Then his mother called him to her side when she was eighty-eight years old. My son, I don't regard you as my son only; you are my teacher: I am not ready. Please prepare me for my home-call. My time is near. Bakht Singh shared with her from the Scriptures, and just before she passed away, he asked her, "Mother, your time is near, are you ready? Do you have peace?" With great peace shining on her face, she passed away. Some of his siblings also received the Lord and were baptized, and others had great respect for the Lord and Bakht Singh and perhaps someday will make a commitment to the Lord.

Bakht Singh at CMS in Karachi

Bakht Singh lived with his sister until she turned him out of her home. Then the Lord opened another door for him, providing a room at the Church Missionary Society compound. He took his meals with whoever invited him: "Breakfast in one place, lunch in another place, and dinner somewhere else. Whoever invited me, I would go happily and eat what was given to me with thanksgiving."

In 1933, Bakht Singh and his co-workers went out on the streets of Karachi making contacts, selling gospel booklets, and giving out tracts to people. One day, Bakht Singh offered a tract to a man called Lekhraj who said to him, "Why do you give us these tracts? First go to your own Christians and change them." He went on, "In which way are they better? We have no peace, they have no peace; they smoke, we also smoke; we go to cinema, they go to cinema; they fight, we fight. How can you say you are better? Show me one really good Christian in all of Karachi and I will become a Christian."

What a challenge! At that time there were more than eighteen thousand Christians in name in Karachi—five thousand Protestants and thirteen thousand Catholics! How could Bakht Singh show him one real Christian in that extremely worldly place? He began to fast and pray every Wednesday by the seaside, saying, "Lord, that man gave the challenge and You give me the answer." A colleague joined him, and they prayed the whole night for the salvation of nominal Christians in Karachi and for the conditions in Punjab. They prayed this way for two or three years.

Extraordinary Prayer Brings Extraordinary Results

When people asked Bakht Singh what was the secret of his successful work in India, his answer was simply, "Prayer." The work in Karachi began with all night prayer. Soon wonderful things began to happen. About those early days of prayer, one of his co-workers, Raymond Golsworthy, wrote:

> One morning, brother [Bakht Singh] said to me, "Let us go and pray together down on the seashore." I readily agreed and off we went. Brother Bakht Singh seemed to be no stranger to the area, and he took me straight to a stretch of beach that seemed to be more or less unknown to others, and we immediately knelt down in the sand. . . . Then Bakht Singh began to pray, sometimes in English and sometimes in Urdu. I found myself sharing deeply in his burden as he spread out the need of the whole area before God, and pleaded for a merciful entrance of God's light. . . . He remembered by name countless individuals who had asked him to pray for certain, personal needs. His intercessions were sometimes interspersed by pauses, and I had the sense that our brother was somehow "watching God" and listening for His responses. It was indeed a day I shall never forget.[3]

59

Bakht Singh's First Co-worker—Imam Din

In 1934, Imam Din was converted to Christ through Bakht Singh's ministry and became his first co-worker. He was a simple man, yet fearless. He had a beard like the Muslims and would walk into Muslim homes and Hindu temples to sell gospel booklets and share the Lord Jesus. One man thought he was a Muslim and asked him what religion he had been before he became a Christian. He told him, "Sir, I was a donkey."

"You mean to say all those who don't know Christ are donkeys?" Then the man asked him, "Am I a donkey?"

Iman Din replied, "Not you sir, only those who do not know the Lord, they are donkeys." The man was put to shame and bought four or five gospel booklets from him. But he was very simple. One day he came to Bakht Singh to ask for an electric light bulb, which Bakht Singh lent to him. That night he came back to Bakht Singh and told him that the bulb did not work. Bakht Singh went to see what the problem was and found the light bulb hanging from a rope.

Before long, Bakht Singh had a dozen such men: one by one they were born again and became his co-workers. Someone asked Bakht Singh why God was not giving him more educated people as his co-workers. Bakht Singh relied that first he prayed asking God to give him some graduates as his co-workers. "Some graduates did come, but there were no results. But through these simple folk, I have openings among lepers, among village folks, in the streets, and all over."

Spiritual and Physical Healings

He was burdened to pray for the lepers when he saw how they were neglected and exploited for money. They were the scum of society. He and his co-workers prayed through the night for them and their spiritual barrenness. As they prayed, the Lord began to work among them—healing them both spiritually and physically.

Bakht Singh was very happy to see that many souls were turning to the Lord. Even though they were poor and belonged to the low caste, he felt one with them. He used to sit with them, eat with them, and spend hours with them. When they were sick and needy, the Lord healed many of them. That is how the work of healing began, but Bakht Singh never made it public. Years later he would ask the Lord to take away the gift of healing because so many were coming to be healed physically and not spiritually.[4]

The simple faith of the sweepers encouraged him and taught him simple faith, as well. They came for the Bible study and then went back to the slums to tell the same stories to their children and women folk. Thus through them, many were born again in different locations all over Karachi, Punjab, Jhansi, and other places.

From Suicide to Salvation

As Bakht Singh was going through the Bazaar one day, he tried to stop a young man to talk to him, but the young man walked away. Bakht Singh walked after him, urging him to stop and talk but the young man walked faster. At last he asked Bakht Singh, "What do you want?"

Bakht Singh replied that he wanted to tell him about the Lord Jesus and how He had saved him. The man responded, "I don't want your religion. I am sick of life and intend to commit suicide by jumping into the sea."

To this Bakht Singh replied, "Why not wait until tomorrow? A few hours more or less won't make any difference."

They went to a small park, and Bakht Singh read him verses from the Bible. The young man listened and wanted to see Bakht Singh again the next day. Bakht Singh agreed to meet him in the same park, and then, after a further chat, the man could commit suicide if he wanted to. The young man said he felt better and no longer wanted to end his life; now he wanted to know more about the heavenly joy of which Bakht Singh had spoken.

Late one night about one o'clock, Bakht Singh was feeling very tired. As he went to bed, he heard a voice saying to him, "Rise and go out." Bakht Singh answered that he was tired, his legs were aching, and he was feeling sleepy. But the voice came again, "Arise and go out." With much grumbling Bakht Singh put on his coat and went out. As soon as he did, he found two young men walking in front of him. He called them and said, "Please stop. I have something to tell you."

When they came near, Bakht Singh told them how he was going to lie down, but the voice of God told him to go out. Then Bakht Singh opened the Bible, read some verses, and told them of his conversion. One of the men said, "I know God has sent you for my sake. I was unhappy and have longed for a Bible. Could you give me a Bible?" He bought the Bible from Bakht Singh and received the Lord Jesus Christ.

Miracles of God's Guidance

Through prayer, Bakht Singh found out that he must go to a small village about 155 miles from Karachi. He asked a friend to accompany him, and the two men set out on the journey. The language of that province is Sindhi, and Bakht Singh knew only a few words of colloquial Sindhi. It occurred to him that there were many Muslims who knew both Sindhi and Urdu, so he might be able to find someone willing to translate for him. On arrival at the village, Bakht Sing asked to speak with someone who knew both Sindhi and Urdu. They were told there was only one man, and he had died the night before.

They went down to the dry riverbed and prayed for about two hours to ask God what they should do. Then the Lord said to Bakht Singh, "I want you to go and speak in Sindhi."

Bakht Singh said, "Lord, how can I speak in Sindhi? I know only a few words."

But the Lord said, "Go and speak."

The two men went into the village and gathered a small crowd. Bakht Singh told them that he regretted not knowing their language fluently, but when he started preaching, the thoughts and words came; Bakht Singh did not know how.

The next morning the voice came again to him, "Cross the river and go to a village named Bannu." They crossed the river in a boat, and at about sunset they came to the small village. In the village center they sold gospel booklets. A Muslim came, addressing them in anger. "Why have you come to this village? You Christians cannot preach your religion here."

Bakht Singh told him that they had not come there by themselves, but were sent by God. They had heard the voice of God and had come to give God's message. They were not missionaries, just messengers. The man asked them where they were staying. Bakht Singh told him they would be staying there—right where they were standing. The Muslim man then asked about their food. Bakht Singh replied they did not know. Then the Muslim man invited them to stay in his house, and he would invite the people to hear God's message. He even offered to translate for them. Bakht Singh was a little apprehensive and asked God if they should go. God told them not to be afraid but to go with him. The man had a large compound around his house, and after giving them food, he brought chairs out into the compound and sent his servants to call the villagers. The headman of the village translated for them.

After Bakht Singh had finished the closing prayer and all the people had gone home, a Muslim policeman came up and said, "Could I have a quiet talk with you? I have been waiting for more than five years for someone to come and explain to me about Jesus. Somebody gave me a Gospel of Luke that I have read many times. I cannot understand it. I am so thankful you have come to my village." For hours that night the man sat and listened to every word and afterward bought a copy of the Bible in Urdu.

Another time the Lord told Bakht Singh to go to Soldier Bazaar. His friends said that it was too hot; that they should wait until morning. But Bakht Singh insisted they needed to go immediately because someone was waiting for the gospel. A team of six or seven walked the three miles to Soldier Bazaar. Each time they stopped, they were asked to move on by the police who told them, " You cannot preach here." When they passed a Hindu temple, the Lord said to Bakht Singh, "Stop here."

They stopped and begin singing songs and preaching. A man came running from the temple. "God has sent you for my sake. My name is Amarnath. I am a graduate from Punjab University. I have been going about in search of peace for four years. I still have no peace. Kindly help me. I have been longing to talk to a Christian, but do not know where they are and how to find them. When I heard you singing, I felt in my heart that you had something for me." Soon he was born again.

From that time on, Bakht Singh decided where to go, when to go, and how long to go only by prayer and waiting upon God.

Crucible of Testing

The most barren part in India for missionary work was Sindh. For about seventy years no work had been done there. It was to this barren region that the Lord led Bakht Singh. He and his team spent hours walking from village to village, and God opened the door to many parts of Sindh.

When Bakht Singh and his friends traveled the lonely desert of Sindh to the villages where no missionary had ever gone to preach the gospel, they were not always welcomed. In one village they could not buy food because they were Christians. They finally were able to get a little red rice flour and some of the ghee (melted butter) that was used to feed the camels. It was full of sand and grit.

In Chikarpal early one morning, he heard a voice telling him to send someone with an Urdu Bible[5] to a neighboring place called Jak Baar, a small town on the way from Quetta to North India. Bakht Singh called his friends and instructed them to go to the village and take Urdu Bibles. They said, "But it is a Sindh village and no one will know Urdu. Bakht Singh told them to go, that it was the Lord's desire.

The next day they went to the village with a small box of books. As they were walking in the Bazaar selling the gospel booklets, a young Muslim man came up and asked them for an Urdu Bible. They sold him one, and he entertained them at the hotel with cakes and tea, as his way of thanking them. The man told Bakht Singh later that he had been waiting for an Urdu Bible for many years.

Quetta Earthquake

In May of 1935, Mr. Loughheed invited Bakht Singh to come to Quetta. Mr. Loughheed was a British military officer who was converted to Christ in Australia and had a burden for the people of

Quetta. He said it was like Sodom and Gomorrah. The meetings were held in the military buildings in Quetta, the first week for Indians and the second week for British soldiers. Large numbers of people came from many different places; most had to come on foot or by horse cart because there were no buses. After a few weeks of meetings, Bakht Singh was greatly burdened by the lack of spiritual interest of the people. On the evening of May 31, 1935, Bakht Singh urged the people to come to God, and those who wished to respond and be saved should remain behind for prayer. Fifty-eight people prayed, one by one, with great conviction, repenting and asking God to forgive them.

A little after midnight Bakht Singh was in his tent feeling worn out, but he could not sleep. The Lord told him to pray for those who had gone away without finding salvation. Bakht Singh knelt down and began to pray, "Lord, will you wake them and shake them. Shake them until they kneel down. Those still in their sins, wake them and shake them." Just before three o'clock in the morning, Bakht Singh was assured that God had heard his prayer, and he went to bed with peace.

At three o'clock in the morning everything began to shake. An earthquake! Bakht Singh thought that God was answering his prayer and stayed on his knees praying. His friend next door was actually thrown from his bed; men and women were crying and shouting in the streets. Bakht Singh's friend came into his tent and told him that there had been a terrible earthquake. The walls of the neighbors' houses had cracked, and everything had fallen down. However, nothing had happened to the tent where Bakht Singh was staying. He and his friend continued in prayer until 5:00 in the morning, asking God to save the souls of those who desired to be saved. Then they went out to see the damage.

It was a sad sight. All the buildings, mud, stone, and brick had crumbled and were in heaps. People were everywhere, some hanging head downwards, some with legs and arms cut off. In all, fifty-eight thousand people were killed that night. Of all those who had come to the meetings, only two were killed.

Bakht Singh and his friends stayed there for about two weeks, going about giving out gospel booklets and doing rescue work. Those who escaped had to stay in filthy grain storerooms with nothing to eat, no shop to go to, and no clothes to wear. They had to use any old blanket they could find to cover the children, and some had none. Bakht Singh prayed, "Lord, will you not give us at least four or five old blankets for these poor children?"

The next morning Bakht Singh met a man named Mr. Evans, a military chaplain, who asked him if he could use some blankets. Some military people had sent him brand new blankets. Bakht Singh could take as many as he wanted, so he took seventy-two—all new woolen blankets.

One evening, Bakht Singh saw a mother with her child who was crying very bitterly. She told Bakht Singh that the child wanted milk, but she had none. Bakht Singh prayed, "Lord, this child is asking for milk; tell me where to go to get a cup of milk."

The Lord said, "Go in that direction."

Bakht Singh went in the direction indicated. He met a person named Dr. Oliver, who asked him if he would like some milk, as there was a good quantity in the hospital. So he brought back a gallon of milk instead of just a cup.

The Lord supplied many needs in this way for Bakht Singh. Food was found for a starving lady after Bakht Singh prayed. A woman was in need of clothes for her small child. The Lord sent him in one direction, and he found someone who gave him a parcel of clothing. Without opening it, he gave it to the woman and her child. When she opened it, she found clothing and shoes the exact size of her young child.

One day the Lord instructed Bakht Singh to give a very poor man twelve rupees. Bakht Singh had twelve rupees in his suitcase that he was saving for train fare to Ajmer where he was invited for a convention. He was leaving in two days, so he said to the Lord, "I must go to Ajmer, how can I give this money away?"

The Lord said to him, "This is my money and not your money."

So Bakht Singh took the twelve rupees and gave it to the man. The day came when Bakht Singh had to go to Ajmer. He was not sure what to do or where to go. He thought about going to his sister, looking very sad, and maybe she would ask what was the matter. But the Lord did not allow him to do that. Then he thought he would send a telegram saying that he was sorry that he could not go to Ajmer. The Lord, however, reminded him that he had promised to go, and therefore he should go. He packed his bag and went to the train station. At the booking office a man asked him if he were Bakht Singh. When Bakht Singh said yes, the man handed him an envelope with his name on it. It contained exactly twelve rupees. He disappeared before Bakht Singh could find out anything about him or thank him. But he had the fare to board the train for Ajmer.

Notes

1. Author's interview with Bakht Singh, 1978.
2. Bakht Singh, *How I Got Joy Unspeakable and Full of Glory*, p. 16.

3. Raymond Golsworthy, "He Taught Us to Pray," special edition of *The Hebron Messenger*, September 2000.
4. Author's interview with Bakht Singh, 1978.
5. Urdu is the official language of Pakistan.

Chapter 6

Martinpur and Beyond

1937

Fear not, O land; be glad and rejoice:
for the Lord will do great things.

Joel 2:21 KJV

True biblical revival is the work of God, though God uses men and women to accomplish his purposes. There seem to be prerequisites to revivals: agonizing, prevailing, consistent prayer, a renewed hunger for the Word of God, implicit faith in the Lord, and total obedience to do the will of God. These were evident in the life and ministry of Bakht Singh. He and his team members would spend days, even weeks, in prayer, and God used him in unprecedented ways in the history of the church in India to bring about the revival that swept across the country.

From 1936 onwards the Lord brought about mighty revivals in many villages, towns, and cities from the north of India, Punjab (now part of Pakistan) to Kerala in the south. The revival spread to more than seventy places in the course of ten years. Tens of thousands turned to God as the Lord began to answer the prayers of many who loved and prayed for the people of India: Praying Hyde in the north, Lady Ogle from England, Amy Carmichael, Pandita Ramabai, and many others in India and abroad. Many spent days and nights in prayer for an awakening throughout India in all its provinces.[1]

In January 1936, when Bakht Singh was only thirty-two years old, he was invited to conduct a small camp in a place called Pathankot in Punjab just north of Amritsar. After taking five meetings a day, he went to his room feeling very tired, too tired to pray. He wanted to lie down and sleep. About an hour later, just after midnight, he heard a knock on the door and a voice. Wondering who it could be at that late hour, he asked who was there. There was no reply, only a second and a third knock. Then the voice said, "Get up and pray." He felt so drowsy, he could hardly pray. Sitting on the side of his bed, he said, "Lord, have mercy upon these people." This happened for four or five consecutive nights. He could not sleep but spent time in prayer asking the Lord to have mercy on the people.

The next Sunday after the morning service in an American Presbyterian Church, Bakht Singh invited the people to come back for the evening service. Everyone came back, which was unusual for an evening service in that church. He invited anyone that wanted to share a testimony to come up to the platform. A young girl of nine or ten years stood up and told how the Lord had forgiven her sins and given her grace to repent. She then asked for forgiveness from her teachers and fellow-students. More girls stood up and shared their testimonies. As they were sharing, Bakht Singh continued praying, "Lord, have mercy upon these people."

Suddenly he heard a sound like somebody whipping people. The entire congregation began to weep. Bakht Singh opened his eyes and saw people falling on the floor under the benches, crying and trembling, some rolling on the ground saying, "Lord, have mercy upon me, have mercy upon me." This went on for three or four hours. Bakht Singh said, "We won't close the meeting until all are given an opportunity to repent of their sins and be born again." Ten hours later almost all there were born again.

A similar thing happened at the Presbyterian Mission Middle School in Sangla Hill where Bakht Singh was the guest of a British missionary, Miss Jameson. Girls, less than ten years of age, were sobbing and asking to be forgiven of God for their sins. Miss Jameson herself broke down and wept, rebuked through the testimony of the girls. A total of twelve girls from Martinpur were attending the school. One of these girls stood up and confessed her sins and prayed for forgiveness. She asked everyone to pray for her village Martinpur, which was considered a very wicked village. That was the first time Bakht Singh had ever heard of Martinpur. He asked if he could accompany the girls back to the village and was shocked to learn how much sin was going on among the Christians there.

Revival in Martinpur: Fire Falls from Above

Bakht Singh was invited to conduct meetings in a village called Youngsonabad, near Martinpur. Youngsonabad and Martinpur were known as Christian villages, both started by missionaries.

The foreign missions had helped these people not only spiritually but also by opening schools, colleges, and hospitals to aid them educationally, socially, and economically. Compared to other places, these Christians were fairly well-to-do. But by the 1930s, many of them were second and third generation Christians living immoral lives.

Bakht Singh was hesitant to go to Martinpur because of the immorality: smoking huka—hubble-bubble,[2] drunkenness, the kidnapping of girls, polygamy, harassment of Christians, and numerous court cases. When he arrived at the village, some elderly people smoking under a tree called to him sarcastically, "Who are you, and why have you come here?"

Bakht Singh replied that he had come to pray for the people of Martinpur. They yelled back, "Don't waste your time, nothing will happen here. Many have tried it and have gone on."

But a large number gathered in the school compound to hear Bakht Singh's message. While he was speaking, people were smoking and laughing—mocking and joking. No one seemed interested in the message. Never before had he seen such opposition and ridicule of his ministry.

For four days Bakht Singh prayed. He did not talk to anyone or sleep, even for one night, as he fasted and prayed that God would have mercy on these people. Then he held his last meeting and told the people that he would be going away the next day. As he was closing in prayer, one man standing in front of him fell down. Bakht Singh thought that he had been stung by a scorpion. Then another fell down, and a third, and a fourth. Soon all the people started to roll around on the ground, pulling their hair and beating their chests and crying out, "Oh Lord, have mercy on me: I am a great sinner."

One of the elders ran up to him and said, "Please stop this!"
Bakht Singh replied, "I did not start it."

This continued on for four or five hours. The people wept and
wept until three o'clock in the morning, repenting of their sins.
A man who was watering his field said that he saw a ball of fire
falling to the earth. When he saw this, he left his field and went
to the meeting without delay. Many cried with great agony, bitter-
ness, and repentance. Both the village pastor and the headmaster
of the school were among those who repented and cried out for
forgiveness.

This went on for the whole week. Conviction among the people was such that they went from house to house, from person to
person, reconciling with each other. People could be seen kneeling
and praying all over the village and fields. The men who had been
smoking and taunting Bakht Singh broke their Huka pipes, burned
them, and spent the whole night in prayer.

A thanksgiving service and love feast were held, and over three
thousand people came. People joyfully brought what they had,
and there was no lack. The village turned into a village of love
and peace. Bakht Singh stayed on for several weeks in Martinpur,
conducting Bible studies and special meetings. The villagers made
a bonfire, burning everything that was not of God. Bakht Singh
wrote about the love feasts years later in the *Hebron Messenger*,
December 25, 1983:

> We decided to have [another] love feast at the end of
> these meetings. When the news of a love feast went round
> in the neighboring villages, we had almost double the
> number of [people], which was more than 5000. . . .
>
> After the meeting, and before they started serving
> the food, I prayed, "Lord, bless the food and multiply it."

We told the people that they could eat as much as they wanted; there was no restriction. They were all filled, and still much food was left over. We distributed it to all who came late. Since then we have had several love feasts after revival meetings, and we announced that all should stay for food after the meeting. There has never been any shortage of food anytime. . . .

The spirit of revival impacted almost everyone as it permeated the life and behavior of the people. One could see evidence of the spirit of prayer everywhere, no matter where, whether it was in the fields or in school. People of all ages where praying day and night.

For several weeks following the revival, about seventy young people on their way to Sialkot for a convention went from village to village preaching the gospel. They went singing and praising God and trusting him for every need. They stopped in every village along the way, singing, sharing their testimonies, and proclaiming the gospel to those who came to listen. They ate whenever someone gave them food and slept wherever they were given shelter. The message spread to about thirty-five or forty villages.

At one village an old man asked Bakht Singh to pray for rain. Bakht Singh knelt down and said to the Lord, "Lord, the old man says he wants rain. Please send rain."

Some were worried, saying, "But we have no umbrellas." Bakht Singh said that he could not change his prayer. Soon the rain came, and they had to walk in the rain to the next village for their meeting.

News spread, and from then on people began to invite them to come to their villages. Along the way, people were healed. When they arrived in Sialkot for the convention, people lined both sides of the road. As they marched through the village sharing the gospel, people on both sides of the road said, "Please pray for me. Please pray for me." There were Muslims, Hindus, and Christians.

How to pray for everyone? Bakht Singh would just pray, "Lord, have mercy on these people and heal them." Many were healed instantly. The news of the revival and the miracles began to spread. Bakht Singh, who had been an unknown itinerant preacher, had now become a household name among the Protestant Christians across India.

Sialkot Convention

In 1937 following the Martinpur revival, Bakht Singh and the young people who went with him electrified the convention by their presence and participation.

The Sialkot convention was started in 1904 by Praying Hyde and others after years of prevailing and persevering prayer. They wanted to experience the deeper life in Christ. By the thirties the Sialkot Convention had become the largest Protestant convention in North India. It was well-known all over the country. Several thousand attended this annual convention, including lay people, pastors, and bishops from many different denominations. When Bakht Singh first attended the convention in 1933, Bishop Bradley of the Methodist Church of Bombay was scheduled to speak, but because he could not arrive in time, they suggested that Bakht Singh speak instead. So from 1933 to 1940, Bakht Singh spoke at the convention, and from there he was invited to many towns and cities. As we will see in the following chapters, Bakht Singh's ministry spread into many parts of India and abroad.

Notes

1. J. Edwin Orr, *Evangelical Awakenings in Southern Asia* (Minneapolis: Bethany Fellowship, 1975), pp. 108–109.

2. One kind of locally made pipe for communal smoking.

Chapter 7

Revival across the Sub-Continent

The word of the Lord spread through the whole region.

Acts 13:49 NIV

Following the revival in Martinpur and his preaching at the Sialkot convention that year, Bakht Singh's name spread across the sub-continent of India. Everyone wanted to hear this young, fiery, fearless outspoken Sikh convert to Christ who preached the Word with power and authority. Sinners were converted, saints were strengthened, and the sick were healed at every meeting.

Bakht Singh zealously spoke against any teaching or practice that he thought was contrary to the Word of God: modernism, the Oxford Group,[1] syncretism,[2] religious pluralism,[3] and other teachings he considered liberal.[4] In the late 1930s, India's struggle for political independence had reached its zenith. Mahatma Gandhi, who was revered and honored not only as the undisputable leader of the political freedom struggle but also as a saint, had acknowledged Christ as a supreme model of passive resistance and a great moral teacher of the Sermon on the Mount but not as the only Savior of the world.

Mahatma Gandhi's Influence

Gandhi had long believed that all religions were merely different roads converging to the same point and considered conversion from the religion of one's birth to another an offense. He disapproved of Christian missions that went beyond social work into the realm of such religious teachings as commitment and confession.[5]

Some thought that Mahatma was greater than Krishna, greater than Buddha, Mohammed, or Christ, for he had in him the combined goodness of all four. "If Christ were again incarnated, he would come just as Gandhi has come."[6] Mr. Gandhi wrote his own religious outlook: "In my religion there is room for Krishna, for Buddha, for Christ, and for Mohammed. I felt that to me, salvation was possible only through [the] Hindu religion. I find solace in the Bhagavad Geetha and Upanishad that I miss even in the sermon of the mount."[7]

Men such as Bishop Henry Whitehead of the CMS Church of South India admired Mr. Gandhi and elevated his stature to almost that of Christ himself. "I frankly confess, though it deeply grieves me to say it, that I see in Mr. Gandhi the patient sufferer for the cause of Righteousness and Mercy, a truer representative of the crucified Savior than the men who have thrown him into prison and yet call themselves by the name of Christ."[8] In the shadow cast by the towering personality of Mahatma, many national and foreign missionaries were reluctant to preach the exclusive claims of Christ for the salvation of mankind.

At the 1938 International Missionary Counsel Conference at Tambaram, a new generation of Indian clergy and laity were highly critical of Western mission. ". . . a new generation at Tambaram, content to preach Gandhi's ethical Christ of the Sermon on the Mount and to engage in Christian charitable projects but increasingly reluctant about preaching the Supernatural Christ of the Cross, i.e., atonement for sin, the resurrection and Pentecost. A church for social reform rather than evangelism was the goal and symbol of this new attitude."[9]

Undaunted and uncompromising, Bakht Singh traveled across the nation preaching Jesus Christ as the only Savior and called people to repentance in the light of the Word of God. His outspoken stand for Christ on the basis of the Bible was often misunderstood and severely criticized by both liberal and evangelical denominational leaders. Even some of the evangelical missionaries were highly critical of him and turned against him. "I was surprised and shocked to find how the evangelical missionaries I met froze when I spoke of him and accused him of being anti-white," wrote Norman Grubb.[10]

Revival in Poona

Invitations for special meetings had come from various parts of India, including Poona. After much prayer to find the Lord's perfect will, he went to Poona in April 1938. He and those accompanying him knew no one in the region. They planned no large meetings there but depended on God to guide them.

Bakht Singh and his friends felt a great burden to pray for Poona after seeing the sad condition of the Christians there: full of strife, worldliness, unbelief, and indifference. Only about twenty people came to the first few meetings held, so they decided that they would spend a whole night in prayer to claim God's promises. When Bakht Singh made the announcement, one of the committee members said he did not believe in such kind of prayer and told the watchman to lock up the church building. They began to pray anyway outside the building in an open space. As they were praying, the people passing by were curious and came to see what was happening.

The next Sunday the meeting held at Christ Church of the Presbyterian Church of Scotland was packed to capacity. A revival broke out when Christians from all the churches started attending. The meetings continued for more than a month, and many were saved. Thousands of Christians took part in a gospel procession through the main streets of the city, singing, praying, witnessing, and distributing tracts. That part of the city of Poona had never witnessed anything like it before. This was the beginning of the revival in the Maharashtra area and, subsequently, to the establishing of New Testament churches.

Nineteen Nights of Prayer

The Lord burdened Bakht Singh and members of his team to go from Poona to the Pandita Ramabai Mukti Mission at Kedgaon for a time of all night prayer. Everyone at the mission—about three hundred of the staff, children, and adults—joined the special time of all-night prayer. Bakht Singh divided them into various groups, with each group praying for revival in different parts of India and other parts of the world. It went on for nineteen nights, almost consecutively. A revival broke out in Mukti, many were born again, and many were healed, both spiritually and physically.[11] Bakht

Singh believed the reason for the unusual blessing at his meetings in Madras and other southern parts of India was due to the whole nights of prayer at Mukti. He particularly noted that the prayers of the women opened up heaven in an unusual way.

Through the revival in Poona, the Lord opened other parts of Maharashtra, Gujarat, and South India. At the invitations of many churches, he traveled all across the area speaking to the large groups who had come to hear him. At one large gospel convention, Moses Dawn of the Assemblies of God was Bakht Singh's interpreter. When the missionary from Moses Dawn's church became concerned about the large numbers of his congregation attending Bakht Singh's meetings, he told Moses Dawn not to interpret for Bakht Singh any more. But Moses Dawn had a vision. In the vision he saw a field ripe for harvest and a man harvesting grain. The reaper, he noticed, kept on moving from a northerly direction as he reaped. Moses Dawn thought, *"How can one man harvest such a big field of ripened grain?"* Then he heard a voice saying, "You join him in reaping the grain." Moses Dawn stayed with Bakht Singh, became a good Bible teacher, composed songs and choruses, and interpreted for him until his death in 1977.

Madras

Bakht Singh again traveled to Madras where he held meetings for nineteen days at the Methodist Episcopal Church. R. R. Rajamani had this to say about his first meeting with Bakht Singh:

> But here was a lean, unimpressive young man with neither moustache nor beard, nor dressed up like a great preacher in tie and collar, and no shoes either, but barefoot and simply clad. I felt sure that, just as I had been disappointed in so many preachers before, so I would

now be disappointed in this man also. At that moment he said, "Let us pray." The huge crowd who were present knelt down and out on the fringe I, too, got to my knees. But somehow, as I knelt with the praying throng, that man's prayer went deep into my heart. . . . If a man can pray like that, I thought, he must truly be a man of God.[12]

During those nineteen days, Bakht Singh's great burden was to speak on prayer. Everywhere he challenged people to pray, especially challenging them to spend time in all-night prayer. Several joined him for a night of prayer at Red Hills Lake, praying for the city of Madras. As a result of those prayers, Bakht Singh spoke to tens of thousands of people. Many were born again or rededicated their lives to the Lord, and lives were transformed. One such man, Rajamani, went from being a discouraged Christian to a man God would use in the city of Madras to do great things and carry on in the revival work long after the departure of Bakht Singh.

Prayer meetings started here and there all over the city. Groups met for prayer at midday as well as in the evenings. In several places all-night prayer meetings were arranged on Saturday nights, and hundreds attended them. The spirit of supplication was upon people as never before. People came under great conviction of sin, and many turned to the Lord. The great revival of prayer continued for two years from 1938–1940. It created much hunger and thirst after righteousness in many hearts, not only among folk in Purasawalkam and Vepery where it began, but in other suburbs of Madras also.[13]

Jhansi

In Jhansi, a small girl asked her father to take her to Bakht Singh's meetings, but he would not. Later he changed his mind and decided to take her. When Bakht Singh got up to preach, he had no message to give. He prayed and prayed, but he felt blank. He told the congregation and four hundred of them began to pray and sing, but still no message. They continued in prayer.

While they were praying, the father of the little girl got up and said, "Because of me you have no message. I am a wicked man. I am a drunkard. I have tried to kill my wife. I did not want to go to the meetings, but my daughter insisted that I come here. Just to please her, I came. God told me to carry my Bible, but I have no Bible. God spoke to me that I was a great sinner, and because of my presence in the audience you could not preach any message."

Saying this, the man sat down. After hearing the man's confession, everyone began to weep. The man prayed with tears to receive Jesus. That was the beginning of the revival in Jhansi. Schools were closed so they could have meetings morning, midday, and evening through the whole month of October.

Return to Madras

In answer to the prayers of many in Madras, Bakht Singh stopped in Madras on his way to Punjab. About that visit that shook Madras, Rajamani has this to say:

> At the beginning of 1940, Brother Bakht Singh passed briefly again through Madras on his way to the Punjab. We were resolved to make the most of the occasion, so we organized a special procession of witness on the Saturday afternoon. A huge crowd gathered until it became the largest such gospel procession Madras had

ever seen. Walking three abreast, the children alone occupied about a furlong (220 yards). The whole procession extended to a mile in length with more than ten thousand people taking part, all singing out. . . . All the denominations joined in, and when we all reached the Methodist Church compound, Brother Bakht Singh gave us a stirring message.[14]

Many in Madras strongly felt the Lord had chosen Bakht Singh to do a new work there. With that in mind, they continued their prayer to the Lord that Bakht Singh would return to Madras. Rajamani said, "Indeed, I now believe that if, like Jonah, he had declined to come to Madras and had gone elsewhere, God would have used some kind of fish to collect him and bring him to us!"[15]

Finally in July 1940, Bakht Singh came back to Madras for a three-month special campaign. He came with a heavy burden to preach on the importance of the Word of God. During the three months, he preached in almost every denominational church in the city, with thousands attending every meeting.

At the beginning of almost every meeting, the congregation was asked to display their Bibles by raising them above their heads while singing a Bible chorus. If they did not have one, Bakht Singh would say, "You should feel ashamed 174 times, because in Psalm 119, out of 176 verses there are 174 references to the Word of God, and if you are a pastor or Christian leader, you should feel ashamed twice more, that is 348 times." Those who did not have Bibles were encouraged to buy their own. Hundreds of Bibles were sold at every meeting with the co-operation of the Bible Society until Bibles in all the major languages of the region were sold out. When the Bible Society sold out of Bibles, people went looking for them in used bookstores.

Wherever he went, large numbers crowded in to hear him. One night the crowd was so large that many could not get in. In order to make more room for people to sit, Bakht Singh requested the benches be moved aside so that people could sit on the floor. He also told the children to come up to an area in the church sanctuary where only ordained ministers were allowed to go. This shocked the church elders, and they reported it to the bishop. Bakht Singh challenged them: "Bishop or no bishop, the Lord has sent me to preach and I must deliver his message. Don't you adults smoke and indulge in other things that defile the house of God far more grievously than the presence of these innocent children in the church sanctuary?"

He was bold and outspoken, fearing no man. He spoke against worldliness, carnality, and hypocrisy among Christians, both clergy and laity. He taught the people to respect and honor God. At one meeting he saw a man in the congregation smiling across at the women. He stopped speaking, walked to where the man sat and rebuked him sternly. He did not allow anyone to behave in a way he thought unseemly in any meeting, whether adults or children.

Wherever he preached, the people flocked to hear him. No notices or handbills were necessary. He would have none. He believed that God's work needed no human publicity. Instead he relied on prayer. The news was passed on by word of mouth, and people came by the hundreds. Even though those were the early days of the Second World War and people were facing many practical problems, large numbers came nightly to meetings that would last for three to four hours, many of them standing for the whole time.

There were many answers to prayer and many healings. A man with leprosy was completely healed with no trace of the disease.[16] Parents brought their child with leprosy that no doctor had been able to cure. After Bakht Singh prayed and anointed the child with oil, the child was healed immediately. The parents and relatives thanked God for the healing and became followers of Jesus. There were many other cases of physical healing, but Bakht Singh never publicized them or held a healing campaign.

Another characteristic of his ministry was the gospel procession. On Saturday morning there would be processions of witness in which pastors and congregations took part, often several miles in length and, at times, numbering more than twelve thousand. With children leading, women following, and men at the rear, they passed through the streets singing. You could hear people singing throughout the city.

Towards the end of his three months campaign in Madras, Bakht Singh announced that he would have a united love feast, and all were invited to come. He asked families to bring enough food for themselves and for one extra person. All were asked to come singing to the place of meetings. The following is a description of the experience:

> Accordingly, that morning, I started out with my wife and three small children. We put our food in a rickshaw and walked beside it in single file. I played on my violin. Navaneetham, who was one with me in everything, joined me as I sang at the top of my voice, and the children added their voices to the chorus. Everybody in the neighborhood knew us. No doubt they thought I had gone mad. As we walked along singing, others bound for the same meeting came out of their houses and joined us. . . . It is hard to believe now that such things really happened. . . . More than twelve thousand gathered on the open *maidhan* (playground) for the love feast. When

we reached the hall, I went into the building to see how the contributions of food were being stored. Volunteers were emptying the baskets of rice into a room. I could not believe my eyes. There was a huge heap of rice, already cooked—and the best kind of rice too. Then I looked at the cutlets, another great heap. Elsewhere other volunteers were already preparing the vast quantities of *sambar* (curry with lentils and vegetables) needed for so great a crowd.[17]

Bakht Singh then asked volunteers to serve the food, and two hundred came forward to serve.

Several hundred attended the all-night prayer meetings, and many came under conviction of sin, confessing with tears. One evening they had a large bonfire to burn things such as sinful books, magazines, photographs, and other articles connected with sin.

Bakht Singh challenged the people to love and obey God above all. One time a newly converted Hindu girl was challenged by his message on believer's baptism and asked Bakht Singh to baptize her. This created a new situation because neither Bakht Singh nor his team members had ever baptized anyone. Moreover, many denominational leaders were opposed to believer's baptism. Meanwhile several others asked if they might be baptized too. Bakht Singh met and prayed with fellow workers, and it was eventually agreed that all, including the girl, should be baptized.

People were encouraged to live simple, holy lives in Madras. For example, many of the men wore plain white shirts, and the women white saris, the white symbolizing holiness and purity.[18] During those days, white saris came to be known as "Bakht Singh saris" and often sold out as they were in great demand all over Madras. He also challenged his listeners to live lives of holiness and separation from the world. He wanted believers to express their separation outwardly by not wearing jewelry or showy, colorful, expensive clothes. He felt that these were signs of worldliness.

A man who later became an elder in one of the churches invited Bakht Singh to his home for a meal. When Bakht Singh saw all the jewelry his wife was wearing, he told her that unless she removed it all he would not take food in her house. She and her husband prayed about it, and she decided to remove it. Later they brought it all to Bakht Singh to be sold and the money used to pay for Bible distribution.

Another time a Christian brother invited him for lunch. This man did not think his house was good enough, so he held the lunch at his son's house. When Bakht Singh saw cinema pictures of partially clothed women hanging on the walls, he asked the man to take them down. "Is this a Christian home?" he asked. "If you do not take these down and destroy them, we cannot eat here." The man was proud and would not take down the pictures, so Bakht Singh left without touching the meal.

Following the three months of special gatherings, before they left for Punjab, thousands gathered at the central station in Madras to see him off. The train had to be delayed; he could not reach his compartment because of the crowd.

Revival in Gujarat, 1941

The revival in Gujarat demonstrated God's work and grace once again. Almost two thousand people sat night after night from eight o'clock until midnight and then had to walk home carrying sleeping babies and leading sleepy children because the buses had stopped running at ten o'clock. There were many conversions and confessions of sin. The whole Christian community was affected, and the revival fire spread to towns and villages throughout the area.

Bakht Singh was asked to come for special meetings at an historic campground for the Gujarat Synod of the Alliance Church. Beside a great many people from the Alliance church, many Gujarati-speaking people of other denominations came. The days began at five in the morning when a bell rang calling people to pray in the church. There were meetings lasting throughout the day and late into the night.

On Sunday morning the church was crowded so that every available space on the floor and the platform was taken. After the message, the Lord's Supper was served to the large audience. The service was conducted with the aid of ten pastors and two elders. The afternoon meeting began at three o'clock, while people were still coming in crowds from the city by train. The church was packed and overflowing. As Bakht Singh's message, "The Necessity of Being Born Again," came to an end, people all over the church stood almost en masse in response. When Bakht Singh prayed, it was as if the Spirit of God fell upon the audience and all, simultaneously, began to pray in earnest. They prayed with outstretched hands or on their faces before God. Some described it as sounding like a "great Niagara of prayer." According to one report, Presbyterian and Methodist pastors led in singing a Salvation Army hymn about "cleansing by the blood of Christ" at the top of their voices. No one left to go home. All were there—Methodists, Presbyterians, Episcopalians, and Salvationists in an Alliance camp meeting—all seeking God.

The meeting lasted until 1:30 in the morning. The rest of the time people gathered to talk about the meeting, and what God had done for them, or to pray together. Finally in the morning light, the people began to go home.[19]

Similar revival broke out in many other places. This was going on while the British Raj in India was coming to an end. In 1941 Bakht Singh returned to Madras as he felt God was directing him to do. We shall see the impact of the revival and the beginning of a new work in the next chapters.

Notes

1. The Oxford Group, or Moral Re-Armament, was a religious movement founded in 1921 by F.N.D. Buchman, an American who defined its aim as a program of personal, social, racial, national, and supernatural change. The Group claimed to be neither a church nor a religious institution. They used techniques to vitalize the members of any religious faith and promoted moral perfection with the Four Absolutes: honesty, love, purity, and unselfishness. In the 30s and 40s in India, many Christians, both clergy and laity, were influenced by this group, and this was a great hindrance to the gospel. W.H. Clark, *The Oxford Group—Its History and Significance*, pp. 26, 30, 153.

2. Combining teachings from various religions, both Eastern and Western.

3. All religions lead to the same goal.

4. Particularly the theology of German theologian Rudolf Bultman's book, *New Testament and Mythology* (1941) heralded the beginning.

5. Susan Billington Harper, *In the Shadow of the Mahatma—Bishop V.S. Azariah and the Travails of Christianity in British India* (Grand Rapids, MI: William B. Eerdmans Publishing Company, 2000), pp. 295–296.

6. P.V. George, *The Unique Christ and Mystic Gandhi* (Tiruvalla Travancore, S. India: The Malabar Christian Office, 1930), p. 150.

7. Quoted in George, 150.

8. Susan Billington Harper, *In the Shadow of the Mahatma*, p. 294.

9. Ibid., p. 242, 293–294.

10. Norman Grubb, *Once Caught, No Escape* (Ft. Washington, PA: Christian Literature Crusade, 1934), p. 150.

11. Mukti Mission was founded by Pandita Ramabai, who was converted to Christ as a young Hindu widow. Later on the Lord led her to establish a home for young, destitute widows and orphans, particularly girls.

12. R.R. Rajamani as told to Angus I. Kinnear, *Monsoon Daybreak* (London: Open Books, 1971), pp. 59–60.

13. Ibid., p. 63.

14. R. R. Rajamani, *Monsoon Daybreak*, p. 64.

15. Ibid., p. 65.

16. Ibid., p. 69.

17. Ibid., p. 63.

18. *Sari* is a piece of cloth measuring six yards (five and one half meters) wrapped by Indian women around themselves as their dress.

19. Jane Elizabeth Kerr, *A History of the Christian and Missionary Alliance in Gujarat State, India* (1942), pp. 37–38.

Part 2

An Apostolic Revival

Chapter 8

Jehovah-Shammah:
A New Beginning

See, I am doing a new thing! Now it springs up;
do you not perceive it? I am making a way in the
desert and streams in the wasteland.

Isaiah 43:19

Our God is a God of new beginnings. While the sun was about to set on the British Raj, the Son of Righteousness was arising brightly in India through the preaching of Bakht Singh.

The goal of evangelism is the church, and the task of the church is evangelism. The Great Commission includes the planting of churches as described in the New Testament. A major purpose of the church is to show forth Christ's fullness, unity, wisdom, and glory. God, who is sovereign, orchestrates everything to fulfill his eternal plan and purpose—for history is his story.

As we saw in the previous chapter, the city of Madras felt the impact of Bakht Singh's preaching and three month campaign. People of all denominations and groups were affected. Families began the habit of morning prayers together, and singing could be heard all over the city. One Hindu man remarked, "It seems as if Madras has become a Christian city."[1]

Special follow-up Bible classes were arranged to feed the new believers and to build up those who had recommitted their life to Christ. Alfred J. Flack and C. Raymond Golsworthy, two young men from London, helped with the teaching. And when the need of accommodations for these studies arose, the Lord miraculously provided a large building, rent-free from a Hindu landlord.

Following the Madras campaign, Bakht Singh went back to Punjab and other places in North India. It was then that a situation arose that would have profound repercussions. Suspicions began to crystallize among local pastors and some western missionaries that their position and authority were being undermined.

Bakht Singh had spoken fearlessly against inconsistencies and hypocrisies he saw in those who called themselves "Christian" but were not living the life of a Christian, especially Christian leaders. He challenged them to do all things according to the Word of God rather than on the basis of men's traditions or man-made church constitutions. To some, his preaching seemed to be arrogant and judgmental. Bishops, pastors, and leaders of some western missionary institutions were offended. They also criticized and opposed the spontaneous gatherings for prayer, Bible study, testimonies, and open-air meetings. They were afraid many of their members were being proselytized by Bakht Singh's preaching. They decided to take steps to put out the fire of revival. In November of 1940, they met and, as a group, closed all of their churches to Bakht Singh's ministry.

Bakht Sing was not overly concerned about the action of the pastors and bishops in Madras. He believed that God would take care of them and help them sort things out. Meanwhile, he felt that his ministry was in the north of India.

In March of 1941, he was physically exhausted by the continuous traveling and preaching. As he was praying, God spoke to him from 1 Kings 17:9, "I have commanded a widow woman there to sustain thee." A few days later a letter from Lady Ogle came inviting him to Silverdale at Coonoor for a time of rest as her guest.

On the way to Coonoor, Bakht Singh would be passing through Madras. He sent a message ahead and asked Rajamani and others to meet him at the railway station. The news of his coming spread like wildfire. Excited about his arrival, the men prayed and decided to arrange a public meeting for him on that day. Their request to hold the meeting was turned down with this statement: "We, in the Indian Ministers conference, have met and passed a resolution to never again make any place available to the Punjabi preacher."[2]

Hearing this the men were greatly shocked and distressed. They prayed and discussed the matter at great length. Many were ready to leave their respective denominational churches. They asked the Lord to guide them and help them find an alternative meeting place.

When the train pulled into Madras Central Station, Bakht Singh was surprised to find such a large crowd of people with their Bibles on the platform to meet him. And on the banner they held up, in blazing letters, were the words, "They shall put you out of the synagogues: yea, the time cometh, that whosoever killeth you will think that he doeth God service" (John 16:2). They all pleaded with him to stay and conduct another campaign. They had found a suitable place were they could erect a large tent, *pandal,* to hold the meetings.

However, he did not have peace in his heart that God wanted him to stay. He was reluctant to hold a campaign without direct leading from God. He also sensed that some of these friends, in their newfound faith, were perhaps a little more zealous than wise and wanted to hold these meetings just to express their defiance. He thus declined to halt his journey at Madras and planned to proceed to Coonoor. But due to the insistence of the saints, he agreed to stop for one meeting.

Bakht Singh spoke for three hours from Psalm 119. He did not mention anything about starting a new work, nor did he encourage them to leave their churches. He had no intention of starting another church for them. He departed for Coonoor, leaving the people in Madras confused and sad.[3] As the train slowly pulled out of the station with Bakht Singh and his team on board, the saints in Madras waved good-bye with tears streaming down their cheeks.

Coonoor

Coonoor is a hill resort nestled among evergreen pines surrounded by the blue mountains of Nilgiris. (*Nilgiri* means blue mountain.) Lady Ogle welcomed Bakht Singh to her palatial home in Silverdale, away from the sweltering heat of the plains with temperatures above one hundred degrees. She made him comfortable and waited on him herself, serving him tea. Lady Ogle had been praying for him; she felt God's hand was upon him and that he was chosen by God to do a new work in India.

Bakht Singh and his team members spent the next forty days praying and waiting on God for direction of future ministry in India, particularly in Madras. With him at Lady Ogle's home were Brothers Flack and Golsworthy. They too wanted to find God's will concerning several matters that were upon their hearts, in particular effective follow-up work and the critical situation in Madras. They were concerned that unless something happened and God intervened, many of the new converts would soon either backslide or fall into false doctrine. Being new, young missionaries, they were greatly concerned that any decision they made would have far-reaching repercussions.

During the ten years that Bakht Singh had been serving the Lord in India, beginning in 1933, he had seen large numbers of new converts backslide within a few months of conversion. From 1936 on, the Lord had blessed him with wonderful, unprecedented revival campaigns in various parts of India. He had seen people trembling and crying out for mercy to God, as they became convicted before Him. They would roll on the floor in agony, hiding under the pews and benches in terror because of their sins in the sight of God. When the power of God was released in a meeting, it would seem as if a mighty unseen hand was thrashing the people with a whip. They would beat upon their chest as they cried out to God for forgiveness. There would often be hundreds, even thousands, of converts at those meetings. Many seemed to be gloriously transformed as a result. But often when he went back to visit, perhaps a year later, the new converts were hardly to be seen. Of the thousands who responded to the gospel message during the revivals, only a few were still going on with the Lord.

For years he thought of himself as an evangelist, responsible simply to evangelize and lead people to Christ. He thought his

personal responsibility ended with the revival meeting, Bible studies, and prayer fellowships. Now a new concern lay heavily on his
heart—what to do about these new converts.

Bakht Singh spent many sleepless nights wrestling with the
Lord to know His will in these matters, and the Lord gave Bakht
Singh a never-to-be-forgotten time at Coonoor. It was destined by
God to revolutionize his life and ministry.

Bakht Singh and those who had gathered with him at Coonoor
began waiting on the Lord. They prayed for many hours, long into
the night. They decided that, rather than spending time discussing
their problems, they would spend the time on their knees praying.
They prayed one by one, asking God to reveal his plan for them
in India and in Madras, particularly. Bakht Singh began reading
through the Acts of the Apostles. As he read, the Lord showed them
that evangelists had a responsibility, not only for the conversion of
sinners but also for their spiritual growth. They realized that the
Great Commission was not fulfilled merely with the saving of souls.
Jesus had commanded his disciples to "go, make disciples, baptize,
and teach" in one inclusive command that must not be divided. It
can be fulfilled in the context of the local church based on New
Testament principles.

As each day passed, Bakht Singh understood more clearly what
the Lord was requiring of him. But the revelation was progressive,
and he was hesitant because he could see quite clearly what it was
going to involve. Up to that point, he had ministered to all and had
been received by all. His desire was to serve all. He could see now,
however, that if they were going to take up the responsibility of caring
for the converts in Madras, it would mean that those who they had
always thought should be responsible for this task—the local pastors
and church leaders—were not going to be very pleased with them.
The result of that would be, almost certainly, more closed doors.

He also had at the time a stack of about four hundred letters from various churches, missions, and individuals with invitations to visit their churches and conduct revival meetings and campaigns for them. He knew if it became known or even rumored that he was associated with a new church movement in Madras, many of these invitations would be dropped.

Bakht Singh found himself locked in a grim impasse with the Lord. At last, one sleepless night, he yielded. Deep in his heart, he knew what the Lord wanted him to do. He got up, rolled up his bedding, and went to prayer, knowing he must settle this matter once for all. He told the Lord that he was ready to do whatever was required of him: "Even if it should cause all my friends to become enemies and all these doors of opportunity to close, and I am no longer invited anywhere for meetings, and I am misunderstood and reviled on every side, I am ready at any price to do Thy will. Only give me the assurance that Thou art leading me."[4]

As soon as he had prayed this, these words suddenly came to him: "Behold, I will do marvels" (Exodus 34:10). It was as if someone was standing beside him, saying to him, "I will do marvels; I will do marvels!" As Bakht Singh continued to pray that night, God directed him to read the words of Acts 26:19: "I was not disobedient unto the heavenly vision;" and 28:30–31: "Paul dwelt two whole years in his own hired house, and received all that came in unto him, preaching . . . those things which concerned the Lord Jesus Christ, with all confidence."

From these words he felt the Lord wanted him and his co-workers, first, to rent a house in Madras and, second, to be freely available at all times to those who would come desiring to know more of salvation. God gave him more than seventy other promises of Scripture confirming His will that they should begin a new work. To be really sure, he spent twenty-one days in fasting and prayer, along with some of his co-workers. In the end, Bakht Singh fell on his face and said, "Lord, I will go to Madras," and as he did so, his heart was flooded with the joy of the Lord. He then asked the others whether they were willing to stand with him at any cost. They all agreed.

Immediately after knowing that it was the Lord's will for them to return to Madras, he informed Rajamani, Dorai Raj, and Rajarathnam that he was coming back and needed them to rent a house for him. While Bakht Singh and his co-workers had been praying in Coonoor, those in Madras were also praying for the Lord's guidance for their future. Rajamani, Dorai Raj, and Rajarathnam had resigned their membership from their churches. They felt for sometime that this was the Lord's plan.

As Bakht Singh and his companions waited for the Blue Mountain train to take them to Madras, they knelt down on the platform and said, "Lord, shake Madras before we reach there." When they reached Madras station, church people were there with posters saying, "Bakht Singh, go back."[5]

The city was hot, and they were tired after their long journey. The rented house was small for the team of about a dozen men, but they made themselves comfortable. Early the next morning, Bakht Singh and his team went out for an open-air procession. The news soon spread about them being in the city. As the procession moved, many joined them and followed them back to their new residence. They crowded into the small house, wanting to know of his future plans for the city. He announced a night of prayer to find out the Lord's plan for the city. An old, dilapidated building in a Muslim cemetery on Pallavaram Hill was located for the night of prayer.

About twenty brethren set out for the night on Pallavaram Hill. Raymond Golsworthy, the young missionary from London writes his personal recollection of the Pallavaram Hill prayer meeting:

The hill was not far from the railway station, and the sun was setting when we began the climb. Soon, it was difficult to pick our way through the rocks and stones, so we lit our petromax lanterns and pressed on. Then came our big surprise! Pallavaram Hill was evidently a favorite haunt for snakes and scorpions! Every few steps, someone would call out that he had been attacked, and we began to wonder whether our choice of a place had been the right one after all! Some even suggested that we turn back and try another day. . . . Brother Bakht Singh, however, urged us to press on resisting, in Christ's name, all enemies that might oppose our purpose—whatever form they might take! By the time we reached the top of the hill, it was quite dark, but we could easily see the bright lights of Madras stretched out beneath us, while some stars were shining on us!

I do not recall the exact sequence of events at that point, but I do know that all of us were very soon on our knees, and praying for the guidance and direction we needed so much. . . . I remember watching the lights of Madras gradually going out, for I confess it was hard to close my eyes! Even the lesser streetlights were switched off, and a strange, and somewhat frightening darkness took over.

By then, it was getting a little cold, so we tightened our shawls around our shoulders while continuing on our knees. And, strangely enough, we felt an increasing closeness to our Blessed Lord. Physical weariness seemed to disappear from us and, again and again, we just had to burst out in our happy songs of faith. Hour after hour, the prayers and praises continued, and we just knew that we were being heard. Then came the moment I shall never forget!! I confess that I opened my eyes, and out on the Eastern horizon, a tinge of light appeared, and then, very slowly, increased. Not long after that, I saw a small crescent of the sun itself "peeping up" over the Eastern horizon—as if it had a message for us! It slowly increased in size, and soon the complete sun was lighting up the familiar Bay of Bengal, and turning it to gold! Soon we could see the outline of Madras itself; our Madras—welcoming the dawning of another day! . . .

It was getting slightly warmer now, and we on the hilltop could loosen our shawls from our shoulders, but still continuing on our knees. Prayer, however, was giving way to praise, and enquiries became "thanksgiving of faith." We had met God and He had put something of His mind deep into our hearts. . . .

What I had viewed from that Pallavaram hilltop was something clearly symbolic. Human and artificial "lights" were being gradually extinguished, and a "Greater Light" was about to rise—the living Christ, Himself! He would become the very substance of a new "Testimony," and only that could meet the need of the city.[6]

It was as if the snakes, scorpions, centipedes, the insects and other creatures that tried to attack those who had gone up to pray on the hill were sent to remind them of attacks and troubles they would face as they began to do the work God was calling them to do.

About that experience, Bakht Singh later recalled, "These scorpions and centipedes were attracted by the bright petromax lights which we had taken with us. We went on killing them as we saw them approaching. It was an unusual experience, because on the one hand we were praying the whole night and on the other hand we were killing scorpions and centipedes. Early in the morning we could see the sun rising on the city of Madras. Then the Lord spoke to us in a clear and open way that we would have to face such bitter opposition and persecution from people that it would be as painful and poisonous as the stings of the scorpions and centipedes. The Lord also encouraged us, saying not to be afraid of them because even though these people may try to harm us, they would not be able to succeed, for as we were able to overcome the scorpions and centipedes, so we will also be able to overcome those who will persecute and oppose us. What the Lord spoke through the scorpions and centipedes turned out to be true.[7]

Through the night of corporate prayer, God directed Bakht Singh and the team to the next step they should take. The night of prayer on Pallavaram Hill was a turning point in the history of Bakht Singh's work. Following that historic night of prayer, in the early hours of Sunday morning, they came down the hill. Though physically tired from a sleepless night, they were invigorated by the presence and the power of the Lord. They read together Acts 2:41 and 42 to find out how early believers worshiped the Lord. "Then they that gladly received his word were baptized: and the same day there were added unto them abut three thousand souls. And they continued steadfastly in the apostles' doctrine and fellowship, and in breaking of bread, and in prayers."

Following showers and breakfast that morning, they met in a school building. And as in Acts 2:41, they had a baptismal service. Sixteen believers were baptized in a small tank adjoining the school. Then Bakht Singh and Brother Golsworthy laid their hands on them, signifying their relationship with them and with the Body of Christ worldwide. Others who had already been baptized came forward for the laying on of hands. Bakht Singh told them that it was their privilege to worship the Lord, and as believers, it was their spiritual birthright to minister to the Lord.

After that all those present spent time in open worship, and all were encouraged to pour out their heart to God. They prayed and sang songs of worship, thanksgiving, and adoration and shared in breaking bread to remember the Lord. Following that, they held a love feast and time of fellowship, demonstrating their oneness in the Lord, regardless of caste, color, and status. It was a significant day in the history of the new work God was doing through Bakht Singh and his co-workers. It was on that day the church we now know as Jehovah-Shammah was born.

Notes

1. R. R. Rajamani, as told to Angus I. Kinnear, *Monsoon Daybreak* (London: Open Books, 1971), p. 69.

2. Ibid., p. 76.

3. Ibid., p. 79.

4. Bakht Sing, *Return of God's Glory* (Bombay, India: Gospel Literature Service, 1969), p. 25.

5. Bakht Singh, *Write the Vision* (unpublished papers, 1966).

6. Raymond Golsworthy, "Pallavaram Hill," Hebron Messenger (July 16, 2000).

7. Bakht Singh, *Come Let Us Build* (Secunderabad, India: Commercial Press, 1975), p. 18.

Chapter 9

Jehovah-Shammah:
To the Praise of God's Glory

Therefore, this is what the LORD says:
"I will return to Jerusalem with mercy,
and there my house will be rebuilt."

Zechariah 1:16 NIV

"Not by might nor by power, but by my Spirit,"
says the LORD Almighty.

Zechariah 4:6 NIV

One of Bakht Singh's favorite sayings was that our God is not
only a prayer-hearing but also a prayer-answering God. Soon after

the night of prayer on Pallavaram Hill in Madras, the Lord led them to a larger place, in answer to their prayers. While they had been praying for a larger facility, Bakht Singh remembered a vision he had at Coonoor some time earlier. In that vision he had seen a house and grounds large enough for their needs. So they began to look around for such a facility.

Captain Manohar found an old building about to be vacated because it was badly in need of repair, and the owner had refused to do anything about it. At first the building and the compound seemed too large for their present need, but the Lord impressed upon them that he had prepared this place and they were to take it.

They approached the owner, a Muslim, and told him they wanted to rent the house and compound for the work of God. Bakht Singh read to him the Scripture God had given him about the place that very morning—1 Chronicles 29:1, "The palace is not for man, but for the LORD God." The owner, Mr. Ishpahani, was impressed and agreed to rent the place to them, and he promised to make all the repairs and even construct a water tank for baptisms. And the place would be rent-free until all repairs were made. At the end of the visit, Mr. Ishpahani knelt with them in prayer and accepted an Urdu Bible as a gift.

They moved in on July 12, 1941, only about three weeks after coming down from Coonoor. They named the building "Jehovah-Shammah," which means, "The Lord is there." Bakht Singh wrote about the vision he had for the work:

> That which would now develop should not be another exclusive body or sect of Christian people, another denomination. It was to be an expression of the heavenly and universal church in its unity and calling. The first

thing to be avoided, then, was a distinguishing name. We knew people would be eager to name us. We knew we would be pressed to name ourselves. Who are you? Where do you belong? What do you call yourselves? You must have a name! All this would come at us from every side.

We had seen that the church of Jesus Christ is already "one new man" (Ephesians 2:14–15). . . . All believers are already united in the "one body." When regenerated by the Holy Spirit they are at the same time baptized by one Spirit into one body. "For as the body is one, and hath many members, and all the members of that one body, being many, are one body: so also is Christ. For by one Spirit are we all baptized into one body, whether we be Jews or Gentiles, whether we be bond or free; and have been all made to drink into one Spirit" (1 Corinthians 12:12–13). It is the expression of this unity that sectarianism and denominationalism has so much damaged and marred.[1] We must be satisfied to be called Christians and not add other names whether human, doctrinal, or ethnological. Any name other than or additional to "Christian" would distinguish us from other Christians and lead to our becoming another sect. Therefore we name the building only, and would be known as believers or Christians, the ones who met for worship at Jehovah-Shammah or at No. 19, Ritherdon Road, Madras. The church is one body, and all believers throughout the world and throughout the ages belong to us and we belong to them.[2]

Bakht Singh emphasized the importance of the body life whenever possible by believers living together and working together under the headship of Christ in unity and oneness. About fifteen believers moved into the facility, both nationals and foreign. Among the nationals were believers from various background, color, caste, class, or language groups. Humanly speaking it was extremely difficult to bring about true oneness and unity in a multi-cultural community; only through the Holy Spirit can such oneness be achieved.

Activities at Jehovah-Shammah were designed to show the spiritual unity of all believers and to help the believers grow and mature in Christ. Man-made barriers were broken down; and all were encouraged to build relationships through the love of Christ.

Strict discipline was maintained among those who lived at Jehovah-Shammah. Bakht Singh was loving and caring and, at the same time, a disciplinarian. One day someone invited Bakht Singh and the housemates of Jehovah-Shammah to a birthday party. Before going to the party, Bakht Singh asked Sam Chacko to stay back at Jehovah-Shammah and keep watch while the others were out. Sam Chacko, who had not had any food and was hungry, tried to sneak into the party to get some food without the knowledge of Bakht Singh and then get right back to Jehovah-Shammah. But Bakht Singh, whose sharp eyes never missed anything, noticed Chacko coming to the party without permission. Bakht Singh asked him why he was not at his post at Jehovah-Shammah, then slapped him in front of all and ordered him back to Jehovah-Shammah for his duty as a watchman. Chacko returned, hungry and sad. After the party was over Bakht Singh, himself, brought food back for Chacko.

Bakht Singh and his fellow-workers believed that the people who came to live and help in the service of the Lord at Jehovah-

Shammah should be trained and equipped through the church there, which they called, "the local assembly." In order to facilitate the training and equipping, a typical day at the facility began with an individual quiet time with the Word and the Lord. Bakht Singh practiced his quiet time by beginning his day at 4:00 AM with Bible reading and prayer on his knees. The day's activities began at 5:00 AM with prayer and breakfast together. At 7:30 AM they would gather for Bible reading and study. An open-air meeting for all who could attend would begin at 9:00 AM. Others were kept busy in the kitchen or with other housekeeping activities. After lunch, there were more Bible studies and prayers. The evening meetings were from 6:30–9:00, followed by an open-air preaching service. Every other Saturday, the people fasted and prayed all night, and Mondays were usually set aside for general cleaning and personal work.

Soon after they moved into Jehovah-Shammah, the large compound walls, both inside and out, were painted with appropriate verses of Scripture in large letters in different colors. The wall of the buildings and meeting halls, down to the toilet facilities, were decorated with Scriptures too. It was like an open Bible. When walking into the compound or the halls, one was struck by the Scriptures everywhere declaring the presence and glory of God.

There was a big banner outside the compound saying, "All are Welcome." People came to Jehovah-Shammah in increasing numbers all hours of the day and night. No publicity was used to draw the people in, but they continued coming, bringing their Bibles, eager for spiritual fellowship over the Word of God.

A few months after they moved into Jehovah-Shammah, a group of pastors from various denominations came to see Bakht Singh and his co-workers. Bakht Singh welcomed them, but soon they began to question him: Why was he baptizing people since he was not ordained to do so, and why had he started another church in Madras? He offered to show them in their Bibles the Scripture from the New Testament about baptism, but none of them had brought their Bibles. Bakht Singh asked them how they were to study the Bible with him if they did not have their Bibles. They left, embarrassed, but promised to come back with their Bibles. They never did.

In the early days they lived together as a family, loving and caring for each other. A story was told about a time when some of the young men came back hungry from an open-air meeting. They went to the kitchen to find food but found only one bowl of rice, barely enough for one person. Seeing there was only one bowl, the first young man gave it to another who might need it more than he. As each one came in, the one bowl of rice was handed to the next one. In the end the bowl of rice remained on the table.

The nationals did not expect any hand-outs from the missionaries. All shared in what they had. This set Jehovah-Shammah apart from other groups who looked to missionaries for their needs. Here the nationals might be just as likely to share what they had with the missionaries. Brother Leslie Carter and his wife were missionaries from England who joined Bakht Singh in 1943 in Jehovah-Shammah. Trusting the Lord for their needs just like the nationals at Jehovah-Shammah, they put what little money they had in the offering box one Sunday. A few hours later, following the love-feast, an Indian brother gave Leslie Carter an envelope. When they arrived home, they found, to their surprise, that the Lord had provided for their needs through the gift of a national brother.

Special provision was made for the recently converted women and girls who had been compelled to leave their homes. Others were there for training in the ministry work. In 1942 they rented a house especially for these women and named it Hephzibah from Isaiah 62:4. Two women from England, Miss Violet M. Green and Miss Grace Stalley, came to help train these young women in ministry work such as house-to-house visitation in their neighborhood. They held retreats for Bible study during the times of public holidays or helped with the open-air meetings. Young women from Hindu, Muslim, and nominal Christian backgrounds lived together at Hephzibah with love toward each other and, as a result of that love, attracted other young women to give their lives to Christ.

Practice and Order

As soon as the believers began to meet regularly, a number of practical matters arose such as maintenance of the work and provision for its progress. There was rent to be paid, and this was only one of the recurring expenses each month. They resolved that they would be content with whatever God gave them, and they would make no appeals nor give any indication of needs they might have. They believed that God would supply all of their needs, if it were indeed his work, without any strategies on their part, and God honored their faith by providing for their needs and financial matters.

Once when they were in need of money to pay bills, a woman gave Bakht Singh an envelope containing a large amount of money. She had been caught in a violent storm on board a ship and had promised God that if he would bring her safely to India, she would sell all of her jewelry and give the money away. God told her to give the money to Bakht Singh, but she had no idea where he was at the time. She finally found him and was able to give him the money in time to meet his need for it.

The Lord also showed Bakht Singh and his co-workers at Jehovah-Shammah that they were not to make any attempt to draw people to the meetings. They were not to advertise or use any kind of publicity whatsoever. They would make only a few brief announcements during the service. Yet people continued to come, not only from Madras and other places all over India, but from Pakistan, Sri Lanka, and other countries.

Every Sunday morning, Bakht Singh and the other responsible men met together for prayer to ask God to give them direction and a plan for the Sunday service that morning. They did not believe in pre-arranged ministry services. Instead, when they met for prayer before each meeting, they enquired of each other as to who had a message from the Lord. Sometimes there would be one speaker; sometimes there would be two or more. They felt that no one should expect to be the preacher at every meeting.

Open Table for All Believers

Bakht Singh and his co-workers believed that the communion service must be an expression of the church as one body. They were convinced that they should welcome all true children of God to partake with them at the communion table without reference to any caste, color, nationality, or sectarian label they might have. If someone were born of God, then he or she was in the same family and should be welcomed equally. From the start, it was their practice to welcome everyone.

The believers met for worship in the main hall of the house, often overflowing to the verandas and side rooms. Someone would open with prayer followed by songs of praise and worship. Most of these songs were composed by Indians set to Indian melodies. Often Psalms were made into beautiful songs of worship set to Indian tunes in local languages. A brief exhortation was given to prepare the hearts of the people to worship. Then for an hour or so the meeting was open to spontaneous worship. Any brother or sister was free to worship the Lord in his or her own language, expressing praise and adoration to the Lord. Some expressed their worship through songs, Scripture readings, or prayers, but prayers of request or petition were discouraged during the worship. The Lord's table was always placed in the middle of the room to show that all had equal access to the Lord and that the Lord was in their midst.

After all had partaken of the communion, there would be intercessory prayer for the church around the world. Then one of the brethren would preach a message from God's Word. An offering was taken as a part of worship, but unbelievers were warned not to give anything. On one occasion, a well-to-do Hindu was in the congregation. When it was announced that unbelievers were not to give any of their money, he was put to shame because he had thought all Christians were only out to get money. He became a believer in Christ as a result.

Following the Sunday morning services, all would be invited for lunch, called a love feast. The love feast helped to break down the wall of caste or social separation that was a major problem even among Christians at that time. Converts from various backgrounds, Brahmins, high-caste, low-caste, and outcastes would sit together to enjoy a communal meal prepared in the Jehovah-Shammah kitchen.

After the love feast, several would head out into the community in a procession of open-air witness. Many would be brought back with them to the evening gospel meeting. Soon there was not enough space for all who were coming to the meetings at Jehovah-Shammah. A pandal (tent) was erected to accommodate the people.

Music was a big part of the life at Jehovah-Shammah. Believers sang to the accompaniment of a harmonium, tablas,[3] tambourines, and other instruments commonly used in India. Moses Dawn, who had served as a Tamil interpreter for Bakht Singh, had put many messages into songs, which were then translated into Punjabi. At the first Holy Convocation, which was held from December 14, 1941, to January 2, 1942, believers from various parts of the country and around the world worshiped and sang together in many different languages. The gospel began to spread ever more widely as the people returned to their homes all over India and the world, talking about the joyous time of singing, worship, and fellowship.

Caring for the Needy

World War II was threatening all around and about to come to Madras. A Japanese invasion of India and Ceylon (Sri Lanka) was imminent. When several ports came under attack from carrier-based bombers, people panicked. Air-raid warnings were practiced and blackouts imposed. Almost all the city churches closed at that time. Missionaries, and even some pastors, left the city.

The believers at Jehovah-Shammah saw no reason to close. They felt it was their task to be available to serve others in time of fear and war. Jehovah-Shammah remained open with meetings every night. Because of blackouts, the roads were dark. Public transportation was closed down, and the buses were dark. Brothers and sisters who walked to the meetings were advised to dress in white and come singing. Some believers were transferred to different places, but this scattering led to increase, for wherever they went they carried the gospel to other evacuees.

In 1943, the threat of war ceased, but another disaster struck Madras. A northeast Monsoon brought torrential rains, flooding low-lying city streets. Power was cut off, badly disrupting communication. Then a big water tank broke sending water like a sea through all low-lying areas. The flood reached the upper stories of many buildings. The house of one of the families from Jehovah-Shammah was in that area. Bakht Singh and others joined in the rescue efforts to help the family escape. Then they went back Jehovah-Shammah to organize rescue and care for the many homeless flocking to Jehovah-Shammah.

Sam Chacko and others who had experience on the water helped with the rescue with boats. Because it was on higher ground, many families left homeless crowded into Jehovah-Shammah for refuge. All who came were fed and cared for. A few went away with a newfound joy in the Lord.

This experience of helping those in need during the flood greatly increased their confidence, as they became involved in meeting real needs. Many lives had been in danger, and the saints, led by Bakht Singh, had thrown themselves wholeheartedly into the task of rescuing them. Some of those who had been helped began to forget their problems with Bakht Singh and their church affiliations. All who came were fed and cared for, regardless of their denomination.

During this time two Muslim sisters, unhappy with their lives, had decided to disguise themselves as Hindus, change their names, and run away from their home. They had been given the name of a schoolteacher, Grace Tangaman, who was to help them become movie actresses. The day they were supposed to go to Grace Tangaman's house was the day of the flood, and Grace's house was under water. Bakht Singh, along with many of his team, rescued Grace and her family. As she listened to the gospel at Jehovah-Shammah, she believed and was saved. When the waters receded, the girls went to meet her at her school. She welcomed them but instead of helping them become actresses, she took them to Hephzibah, the sisters' home connected with Jehovah-Shammah.

The young women, Miriam and Khadija, were frustrated and infuriated. Not only did they feel betrayed, but also a Christian center was the last place they wanted to go. However, when they got to Hephzibah, they were touched by the genuine love and concern of the sisters there. Still, they said they would rather die for their Muslim faith than accept Christianity. One Sunday morning they went to the worship and prayer service. As they listened to the prayers of the sisters, they felt the presence of God. Khadija started to tremble from head to toe. She prayed, saying. "Lord, who is this living God? Reveal Him to me and I will put my trust in you, even if I have to lose my life." God revealed himself to her, and she believed and was baptized. Miriam also accepted the Lord. Later Bakht Singh renamed them Esther and Ruth, and they later married two of his co-workers.

Setting Apart Elders

As Bakht Singh and others studied the Scriptures, it became apparent to them that those who regularly engaged in the ministry of the church should be called elders. According to the Scriptures the elders are the ones who should take the spiritual lead in the life of the local church. They began to pray that God would show them who should be elders. Bakht Singh then asked three of the men to spend time in prayer on their own to see if they should be the ones appointed as elders. Their names—R. P. Dorairaj, George Rajarathnam, and R. R. Rajamani—were announced and the whole church held a week of prayer concerning the matter. When it was confirmed that the church had agreed on these men, a special service was held, and hands were laid on them by Wilfred Durham, a British missionary in Bombay, and Bakht Singh to set them apart as elders in 1944.

Coming to Jehovah-Shammah straight from their offices each day, these men prayed together over all church matters and with anyone who needed spiritual counsel or help. Nothing was done until they were unanimous in their decisions. Often they would wait upon the Lord for many hours and even days as they sought His will on some matter of special consequence. Rajamani recalls how, on one occasion, Bakht Singh was invited to Colombo and had even bought his ticket to leave the next day. As the elders prayed with him that evening, however, one of them could find no liberty in the Spirit for Bakht Singh to leave. Bakht Singh cancelled the ticket and delayed his travel until all were in agreement, united in heart.

Holy Convocations

As mentioned previously, the annual Holy Convocation was one of the special features of Bakht Singh's ministry. The first one, held in Jehovah-Shammah in December of 1941, lasted nineteen days with more than a thousand people attending. A large pandal (tent) was erected, with huge white banners of Scripture verses hung all over it. Accommodations of booths and palm-leaf thatched sheds were provided for the several hundred people who stayed there on the grounds. Breakfast, lunch, and supper were provided each day for everyone, cooked by volunteers in the Jehovah-Shammah kitchen. No one was charged, and no appeal for money was made, yet the Lord met every need. One of the main purposes of the Holy Convocation was to provide fellowship for the scattered believers who did not have a local church or believers to fellowship with regularly.

Bakht Singh emphasized the fact that all believers are members of one spiritual family, thus all were encouraged to meet together daily for morning and evening family prayers. There were ministry meetings in the morning, afternoon, and evening, and special meetings for children, young people, and sisters. The joy of worshiping together in so many languages was wonderful, and the gospel began to spread as those who attended the convocation went back to their homes and neighborhoods, sharing their joy.

Gospel Outreaches

In 1943, the church at Jehovah-Shammah began a door-to-door evangelism campaign. Each evening the men would come directly from their offices to Jehovah-Shammah. After a time of prayer, they would set out two-by-two in different parts of Madras selling gospel booklets and Christian books door-to-door. Their aim was to get the Scriptures into every home in the city. Each day they walked many miles through the city, staying out until midnight when there was a full moon. They had a passion for God and compassion for people to hear the gospel.

Early in 1944, they began a series of "gospel raids." A large group of brothers and sisters would travel together for a visit of several days to places a great distance from Madras. Their aim was to spread the gospel and at the same time encourage and help the local believers in their witness. Sometimes the group would number a hundred or more. They would spend the night in schools and go out in processions through the towns singing songs. While Bakht Singh preached, others would sell gospel booklets or talk with the people.

As they traveled further and further from Madras on the different gospel raids over several years, the work spread in Andhra, throughout the area, other parts of India, and the whole world.

Notes

1. Bishop V.S. Azariah (1874–1945), the first Indian bishop of the Anglican Church at Dornakal, Andhra Pradesh, from 1912–1945, commented over the evils of denominationalism in India. His biographer writes, "First and foremost was his commitment to evangelization and his recognition that denominationalism weakened the effectiveness of missionaries in India . . . the ardent evangelists recognized that denominationalism was a barrier to the effective propagation of the gospel. . . . Worst of all, denominationalism inhibited Indian Christians from overcoming their own prejudices of 'race, language, caste, and social status.'" Initially meaningless sectarian divisions inherited from the West were being reinterpreted, Azariah warned, to reinforce India's indigenous sociological divisions. Denominationalism permitted Indian converts of different castes to preserve and even strengthen their social separations by joining churches of different denominations. Thus, Azariah claimed, "separate castes merge into separate denominations and once more continue their unholy warfare of generations."

    Azariah views the problem of denominationalism in much the same way as his contemporary H. Richard Niebur who identified various sociological determinants of ecclesiastical sectarianism as "the accommodation of Christianity to the caste-system of human society." To Niebur, "the evil of denominationalism" lay in "the failure of the churches to transcend the social conditions which fashion them into caste organizations." Both men regarded church divisiveness as a moral failure falling short of the ideal of Christian brotherhood as presented in the Bible. In *The Shadow of the Mahatma*—Bishop V. S. Azariah, and *The Travails of Christianity in British India* by Susan Billington, Harper, p. 239.

2. Bakht Singh, *Write the Vision* (Unpublished papers, 1966).
3. A harmonium is a manually operated Indian organ. A tabla is a percussion instrument.

Chapter 10

Andhra Pradesh and Beyond

*Arise, shine, for your light has come, and the glory of
the* LORD *rises upon you. See, darkness covers the earth
and thick darkness is over the peoples, but the* LORD
rises upon you and his glory appears over you.

Isaiah 60:1–2

The growth and spread of the New Testament Assemblies in
Andhra Pradesh was astronomical. In less than twenty years, the
Lord raised up through the ministry of Bakht Singh and his co-
workers hundreds of local churches in Andhra and other places
across India and abroad. According to Vern Middleton, a Canadian
missionary to India in the 1970s, the Assemblies founded by Bakht
Singh and his team were the fastest growing churches in India, particularly in Andhra.[1]

Dr. George Peters of Dallas Theological Seminary once visited Bakht Singh in Hebron and told him that he had visited many foreign mission fields in Asia, Africa, and other parts of the world but had never seen such a work as he had seen at Hebron. He then asked Bakht Singh, "Tell me what is your secret or strategy?" Bakht Singh replied that he had no strategy or method. He and his co-workers had no extra qualifications but were simple people without much education. They simply decided to do all things by prayer and in oneness and total obedience to the Word of God, without any compromise.[2]

Although Bakht Singh and members of his team had been evangelizing various parts of Andhra since 1942, the actual church-planting ministry in Andhra began with the establishing of an assembly in Cuddapah in 1945.[3] During the Holy Convocation at Jehovah-Shammah in 1944, Samuel, a believer from Cuddapah, approached Bakht Singh several times in tears with a request for him to visit Cuddapah. Several months later Bakht Singh was able to stop there on his travel from Anantapur to Madras. During lunch at Samuel's house, he asked Samuel's wife and four daughters if they were born again. They stared at him blankly, not knowing what he meant. He shared the gospel with them and the whole family knelt down and gave their hearts to the Lord that same hour.

The Lord showed Bakht Singh clearly that he should go on a gospel campaign to Cuddapah. He was there only one day when a Hindu man came to see him, wanting to know whether he wanted to purchase five thousand copies of gospel booklets in Urdu from him. Naturally, Bakht Singh was suspicious, wondering how it was that a Hindu was selling Christian literature in the language of Muslims. The Hindu man told him they had belonged to a Christian missionary who had died. When the missionary's personal items were disposed of, he bought all the gospel booklets, thinking that he could resell them to the Bible Society. The Bible Society was not interested but suggested he go to Bakht Singh. Bakht Singh's team didn't think they would be able to use such a large quantity of Urdu gospels in South India, but bought them anyway, quite unaware of what the Lord had in mind.

Even though it was a Muslim stronghold, God had prepared the hearts of the people, and as Bakht Singh and his team went around Cuddapah, the people were receptive to the message and begged for copies of the booklets. Soon they had sold all the five thousand booklets.

The Lord used Bakht Singh and his team in unusual ways to spread the gospel message throughout that region. Once as they were traveling back to Madras, Bakht Singh remembered that a believing family lived in one of the stations on the way. He sent a message ahead that he would be traveling through and would stop to visit them on the way. When they arrived, the family met them at the train station and took them to their house. While they were having breakfast together with the family, a man came running in, asking them to come soon for the meeting.

"What meeting?" Bakht Singh asked. He did not know of any meeting and was planning to leave on the next train.

"Please come and see," the man urged. "There are more than a thousand people waiting for you to give them a message."

Surprised, Bakht Singh found out that some pastors of the local mission had apparently become agitated on hearing that Bakht Singh was coming to the area. Thinking he must be coming for a campaign, they sent out a letter warning their people about Bakht Singh. They urged the people to boycott Bakht Singh's meetings. But without mentioning anything to the pastors, the local people obtained permission to arrange a meeting on the railway tennis court. Using bamboo poles and bamboo screening, they had covered the tennis courts, making a fine auditorium where the people were now gathered. Bakht Singh abandoned his previous plans and stayed on for three days in Rajahmundry. As a result, there are still many local assemblies there and in the neighboring areas.

Another time a Hindu man from the town of Proddatur came to see Bakht Singh at Jehovah-Shammah. He said, "Sir, I have heard of you and your people. I am a Hindu and a goldsmith from Proddatur. My wife has been sick for a very long time with an incurable disease and is now in the hospital in Madras. Will you kindly come and pray for her?" Bakht Singh went to the hospital with the man and prayed for the sick woman, staying only a few minutes to share the gospel with her and her family.

A few days later, the whole family of eight walked into the Jehovah-Shammah compound. They told him that the woman he had prayed with in the hospital was now healed. They went on to say that Jesus Christ had spoken to each of them, and they had accepted him as their Savior. All eight members of the family asked to be baptized. This story spread throughout the area, many Hindus and nominal Christians were saved, and several churches were planted as a result.

In 1950 Bakht Singh and his co-workers were invited by some missionaries to speak in the town of Cumbum at a convention organized to commemorate the seventy-fifth anniversary of the beginning of their work. After he and his coworkers prayed about going there, he felt assured by God to accept the invitation.

When he arrived in Cumbum, he found about four thousand people gathered for the convention. During afternoon tea with the leading missionaries, he heard talk of the plan to baptize 222 people during the celebration. This was to commemorate an event that had happened 75 years ago when 2,222 converts had been baptized. Bakht Singh asked if all 222 persons were born again. The missionaries were not sure because each pastor had been asked to send a certain number to be baptized. Everything had been arranged months ago and couldn't be changed, so they were going ahead with the baptism anyway. Bakht Singh was surprised at their answer and began to tell them a story to make his point.

"Suppose a young man comes from the army on a leave and finds his aged father seemingly on his death bed. He is a hundred years old, and he is likely to die in any case. As the eldest son, the young man has the duty to see to his father's burial, but he has only a couple of days left before he must return to the army. But his father lingers on. Since his father is almost dead anyway, the young man decides that, under the circumstances, he will go ahead and bury his father now. He has him carried to the cemetery and buried." Bakht Singh then asked the missionaries what they thought of the young man's actions.

"He should be sent to jail," they said.

"But what about you?" he asked them. "How can you bury in baptism those who in fact have not died to sin?"

"But we have been planning this for many months and cannot change our plans now," was their reply. They also told him that they were planning to show a film before he was to speak. "Do you mind?" they asked him.

"I do not believe it is right to bring people to the meeting to watch a film and then preach the gospel to them. It is like tricking them," he replied. "I do not approve of using the film in this way, but I cannot insist that you cancel it."

But then it began to rain unexpectedly. The monsoon rains had not yet broken, and this was an unforeseen disaster. When the rain did not let up, the men came to Bakht Singh with a proposal. "Will you pray that the rain will stop? If the rain stops, we will cancel the film!"

Bakht Singh accepted the challenge. He prayed and God soon stopped the rain. The film was canceled, and the meeting was held. Bakht Singh used the opportunity to preach about baptism to the Baptist missionaries and their converts, quoting at least fifty-five Scripture references concerning baptism. But as soon as the meeting was over, the rain started again—not ordinary rain but heavy, pouring rain. In the morning one of the missionaries came to him, "God has spoken to us through the rain. The baptisms are cancelled." Bakht Singh saw this event as God opening the eyes of nominal Christians to the folly of following man-made traditions and plans.

Hyderabad

In 1950 Bakht Singh and his team were led by God to Hyderabad. For years, believers in the area had been requesting that he come for special meetings. After much prayer, Bakht Singh along with a party of twenty arrived in Hyderabad. They were welcomed and led in a procession, singing, to the meeting place. Most of the believers were members of the Baptist Church and had obtained, with great difficulty, permission to use the mission facility for the meetings. They were not allowed to stay on the premises, however. So Brother Lawrence, a foreman on the railway, offered them a room in his house. There were twenty of them—both men and women! Bakht Singh remarked that the Lord gave them grace to stay in the limited accommodations. "We rationed the space and slept turn-by-turn."

At every meeting, the building was packed, with hundreds standing in, around, and outside the building, holding umbrellas, not deterred by the monsoon rains. Bakht Singh and his team were planning on staying only three days in Hyderabad, but because of the enormous response from the people and blessing from the Lord, the meetings continued. Hundreds were born again and many recommitted their lives to the Lord. They all expressed their desire to be baptized but the mission refused to take care of them. Therefore, Bakht Singh and his team, after much prayer, decided to hold a baptism.

Among those being baptized were children of Baptist ministers. The Baptist pastor asked them why they were being baptized a second time. They replied that they even though they were children of Baptist ministers, they had been living in sin, not born again, until the gospel was preached to them. Following the baptism, the Baptist authorities refused to let Bakht Singh continue his meetings at their facilities. So Bakht Singh and his team moved the meetings to a large tent. People continued to come, and many were saved. Every Saturday they held a baptism in the lake, sometimes baptizing hundreds. Often Bakht Singh himself did the baptizing.

The work continued to grow, not only for the weekly meetings but also on Sundays. Soon they had outgrown their meeting facility. The team prayed and asked God to do something for them. The Lord answered their prayers by sending a Roman Catholic gentleman, Colonel Ross, who had been converted during one of the meetings. He arranged for Bakht Singh and his team to use, free of charge, a beautiful pavilion designed in the ancient Muslim architectural style. Hyderabad is the capital of a Muslim state and the pavilion had been used for ceremonies by a former Muslim king. It could seat well over a thousand people. Even the electricity and chairs were provided.

They held a three-week campaign in the pavilion. Hyderabad is a large, cosmopolitan city and also the stronghold of Aryasamaj, a militant Hindu organization dedicated to opposing Christianity. One of the days during the campaign, members of this group came to the meetings, intending to start a fight. They were sitting in an area with those who had asked to be baptized. Bakht Singh asked those sitting there, one by one, to tell publicly why they wanted to be baptized, how had their lives and conduct changed, and if they had a good conscience toward others. As Bakht Singh moved through the rows with his questions, the members of Aryasamaj grew uncomfortable and quickly disappeared, knowing that they would be expected to answer the same questions. Hiding nearby were more than forty other members, waiting with weapons for the fight. They left too. God had protected them again.

As the number of new converts grew, Bakht Singh and the team could see that the new believers were going to need shepherding and teaching, and they would have to find a larger place. They began to pray for the Lord's direction. A few days later, a man by the name of Major Paul asked Bakht Singh if he would take in some of the village people. Bakht Singh replied that their place was not big enough to handle any more people. Upon hearing this, Major Paul took him and some of the men to a large vacant building surrounded by three acres, a palace that had once belonged to a member of the ruling class. Looking it over, Bakht Singh thought it was far too good and far too big for them. They knelt down right there and prayed, asking God to make his plan known to them. As they prayed, the Lord clearly spoke to them, "Take it. It is not meant only for Hyderabad City and the area around here. It is for the whole of India." Based on that assurance, they decided to rent it, and Bakht Singh named it Elim. The very next day, the Lord provided the advance money for two months rent. They moved in and held the first Holy Convocation in Hyderabad at the end of December 1950.

The Lord continued to bless them, and the tent set up in front of the house for meetings had to be enlarged three times in as many years to accommodate all of the people. It was common for them to have up to fifty baptisms every Sunday. Until this time, they had presumed that the Lord would take them into parts of southern India. But instead, God had brought them to Hyderabad. Little did they realize the size of the harvest he was preparing in this region.

Hebron

One day several men with Bibles in their hands were walking to a meeting. An old gentleman, secretary to the prime minister of Hyderabad, noticed their Bibles and decided to follow them. Curious about them, he followed them into the meeting. Listening to the message, he became a believer and was baptized. Five years later, he wanted to give his house and compound as a gift to Bakht Singh for the Lord's work. Bakht Singh prayed about it for two years until he was convinced it was the Lord's direction. He accepted it and named it Hebron.

Suitable facilities had to be built on the compound: offices, meeting halls, and facilities for the male and female residents and the constant flow of short-term and long term-term visitors. When these were completed, Hebron was dedicated to the Lord in December of 1959.

Everyone heard about the spiritual atmosphere at both Elim and Hebron. Bible studies, prayers, and spiritual fellowship blessed all who visited. The workers the Lord brought in were from all sorts of background, with diverse talents and gifts. If any of the residents quarreled, they were not allowed to participate until things were made right and the disagreement settled. This made for a harmonious unity throughout the compound.

The work at Hebron grew in amazing ways. During the All India Holy Convocation they accommodated over twenty thousand guests on the compounds. People were "packed in like sardines."[4] They came in spite of all the physical limitations and sufferings.

Bible correspondence courses sent to people all over India is another successful ministry still going on from Hebron. Many from Hindu, Muslim, and nominal Christians background have testified they found salvation and new life through studying the Word of God with these courses. Books, magazines and tracts are also published and sent out from Hebron.

Spontaneous Growth

Did the leadership of Hebron in the late 1950s follow any church-growth strategies or formulas to proliferate the ministry and work throughout India? They were criticized for "starting churches everywhere," and some thought that was their planned strategy. However, the men themselves felt that they were chosen for this work by absolute grace, not because they were worthy or more faithful than others—as if they were pushed along by God. To do anything other than they did would have been conscious disobedience. Nonetheless, a great many churches came into being directly or indirectly from the ministry at Hebron. The men in leadership recognized it as the power of God's message through his Word going out throughout the area.

It was their policy never to interfere in the local churches. They only went to the different areas if the local believers called on them. Many of the churches started up after a few believers from a town or village attended one of the Holy Convocations and saw the "House of God" being expressed. When they returned to their own places, they no longer fit into their old denominational systems and would begin their own church gatherings.

Bakht Singh writes:

> We never preached or taught that the believers should in any way seek to precipitate a "bursting" or separation, but just as people never build houses in graveyards, so the living cannot abide with the dead. Thus we have seen those who had become "new wine" quietly grow together, and the Lord would put them into new skin. It has not come about on anyone's instigation, but rather it has been the spontaneous result of "new life" being experienced and new "vision" being granted. The new life has been so vital and the new vision so compelling that things took their own course locally without our intervention.[5]

According to the need and after much prayer, Bakht Singh would send out one or two bothers, like Paul sent Timothy or Titus, to help with these newly formed fellowships. They were to stay only two or three years, then move on to another fellowship that needed help.

Jordan Khan

The Lord used various people to spread his message across India and plant New Testament assemblies, but the chief among them was Jordan Khan. During the 1940s, when colonial India was going through unprecedented Muslim-Sikh-Hindu riots resulting in many deaths and the eventual partitioning of India into Hindustan and Pakistan in 1947, the Lord brought about reconciliation and unity among the people of the sub-continent of India through the preaching of Bakht Singh, a Sikh convert, and Jordan Khan, son of a converted Muslim.[6] Both were born and raised in Punjab, which is now part of Pakistan and thus were Punjabis. God used these two Punjabi converts, who would have been considered political and religious enemies, together to unite many in India in Christ.

Converted at the age of twenty-one, Jordan Khan resigned his job as a railway employee to work full time serving the Lord. During this time, he came into contact with many who were converted and blessed through the ministry of Bakht Singh. In 1944, he visited Bakht Singh at Jehovah-Shammah. He was impressed by Bakht Singh's life and example of prayer. That was the beginning of a friendship that grew and deepened over the years.[7] After spending several weeks there, Khan went back to Punjab to continue his ministry.

Khan had a deep passion for the Lord and compassion for souls, but he did not take care of own his health or spend any time on himself and his needs. As a result his health deteriorated. In spite of his poor health, he continued to preach, and many were converted. The Church of Scotland invited him to hold meetings in Darjeeling in 1947 and later in Kalimpong[8] and the surrounding areas. Through the resulting revivals, many were converted, new churches formed, and the gospel spread through the region.

In 1948, when the assembly in Kalimpong began, the believers met on the basis of Acts 2:42 under the name Jehovah Nissi in the home of Victor Pradhan. Three months later, they moved to a new site, which they named El-Shaddai. As the need for shepherding new converts arose, Victor Pradhan began to work full-time in the ministry. The Lord used him and others all over Kalimpong, Darjeeling, Siliguri, Nepal, Sikkim, and Bhutan. The 1948 Holy Convocation and the visit of Bakht Singh to Kalimpong stimulated the work of God over the northeastern parts of India, including Hagaland, Mizoram, and Assam.

Nepal had been closed to the gospel for many years. Through the Nepalese who were converted in Kalimpong and Darjeeling, the gospel spread to Nepal, in spite of persecutions, trials, and imprisonments, and through the ministry of Prem Pradhan, who worked closely with the group in Kalimpong. Many New Testament churches were established in Nepal.

In 1955 an evangelistic team was sent to Katmandu, the capital of Nepal. Khan led the team. Right away the team reported to the police what they were planning to do and were given a green light to go ahead. Wearing the national dress, they distributed thousands of tracts, booklets, and gospels and were unrestricted in their preaching. In 1956, a permanent team was sent to Katmandu to set up a fellowship for the new converts. This is the method both Bakht Singh and Jordan Khan used to provide encouragement and strength to the new converts.

Jordan Khan continued to serve the Lord relentlessly both in India and abroad. He worked with various ministry groups and visited many countries as a messenger of the Lord. From the time of his conversion until his death in 1984, he was a flaming fire for Christ in spite of his physical weakness.

There are now hundreds of functioning local churches or assemblies in Kalimpong and Darjeeling districts, Sikkim and Nepal, and in other northeastern parts of India. Ninety-five percent of the new converts are from non-Christian backgrounds—Buddhist, Hindu, animist, tribal, and others. The work and ministry continue to grow.

Notes

1. Based on research done by church growth students under the supervision of Professor Vern Middleton, Yavatmal Theological Seminary, Prune, India (Author's conversation with Vern Middleton in November 2001).

2. Author's interview with Bakht Singh, 1978.

3. Ibid., 1978.

4. The last annual Holy Convocation at Hebron, Hyderabad, was held in 1985. Over 30,000 attended that Holy Convocation. Due to a lack of adequate facilities the Holy Convocation has been cancelled for the time being.

5. Bakht Singh, *Write the Vision* (Unpublished papers, 1966).

6. Jordan Khan was born on February 26, 1918. His father was a converted Muslim who served for a while as a Presbyterian pastor and later became a co-worker with Praying Hyde.

7. See Beulah Yogi, *A Soul's Travail Satisfied; The Life and Testimony of Jordan C. Khan* (New Delhi, India: Masihi Sahitya Sanstha, 2001).

8. Kalimpong is nestled in the foothills of the Himalayas. It is a beautiful place, strategically located northeast of West Bengal, and surrounded by Sikkim in the north, Bhutan at the east end, and Nepal on the west. Because of its location it can be used as a base to take the gospel to all the neighboring areas and countries.

Chapter 11

World Wide Impact

*Your eyes will see the king in his beauty and view a
land that stretches afar.*

Isaiah 33:17

God used Bakht Singh in an unprecedented way during the
first thirteen years following his return to India from the West in
1933. Spiritual awakenings and revival swept across India in cities, towns, and villages from Karachi in the northwest to Kerala in
the southwest. During this time, the news of his ministry spread
abroad through western missionaries who were working in India.
Missionary magazines and newsletters all over the world told of
the revivals and healings that took place in India through Bakht
Singh.

Bakht Singh's vision of the church was not only for the Indian sub-continent but also for the whole world. Some people mistakenly referred to him as an Indian raised up by God mainly for India. His life and ministry show otherwise. While his primary burden was for India, he also had a concern for the church worldwide. He wanted to see local churches showing forth God's glory everywhere. He traveled to every continent as an evangelist as well as an apostle. This chapter briefly tells the stories of some of the people and places in the rest of the world influenced by Bakht Singh's ministry.

Early one morning while he was in Coonoor, he heard a voice saying, "Your eyes will see the king in his beauty and view a land that stretches afar," the words of Isaiah 33:17. The following two mornings he heard the voice again. Finally on the third morning, he asked the Lord, "Tell me the meaning of this verse."

"I want you to get ready to go abroad, to a land far off," he heard the Lord say. He went back to Jehovah-Shammah to share this with the brethren there, and they began praying about it with him. They too had peace that he should go abroad.

The Lord urged him to go quickly. During his daily Scripture reading while reading Ezekiel 8:1—"And it came to pass in the sixth year, in the sixth month, in the fifth day of the month . . ."—he understood that he should arrive in London on the fifth day of the sixth month. He would have to get a passport quickly—in just two days—and he would need money for the passage. Amazingly, he got his passport, but he still needed the money. Then a couple whom he had never met, a Mr. and Mrs. Devasahayam, came to see him. They said the Lord had told them to bring a special gift of money to Bakht Singh. God provided the money in time for him to get to the ship in Bombay.

When he arrived in Bombay, however, he was told that there was no room for him on the *Veronica*, the one passenger ship leaving that day and arriving in London on the fifth of June. But there was room for him on the *Andes*, which was leaving two days later and would arrive in London on the seventh of June. There was nothing else to do but take the later ship. As it turned out, the *Veronica* had engine trouble and was delayed getting to London, and the *Andes*, a much faster ship, arrived in London on the fifth of June.

When he arrived in London, Bakht Singh had no place to go because he had not made any plans but had come only on God's leading. He went to the one place he knew, the assembly of believers at Honor Oak in London. They welcomed him and told him that they had been praying for him for many years. While he was there he received many invitations from churches in various places of England and Scotland. While he was in Scotland, the Lord spoke to him through Zechariah 9:10: "His rule will extend from sea to sea," and Bakht Singh knew the Lord wanted him to cross the ocean and go to North America.

A letter came for him inviting him to be the keynote speaker at the first InterVarsity Christian Students Missions Conference, now known as Urbana InterVarsity Students Missionary Convention, held once every three years on the University of Illinois at Urbana Campus. This confirmed for him that the Lord wanted him to travel across the ocean to the United States and Canada.

It was at the end of World War II and difficult to get passage from England to North America. There were no seats available by ship or by air, but the Lord spoke to Bakht Singh through Isaiah 43:16: "This is what the Lord says who made a path through the sea." He knew then that God would provide a way. The shipping company told him there was no way he could get a ticket. They suggested that the only chance he had was to visit a Mr. Hardy at the British High Commissioner's office because sometimes government servants were given special consideration there. He went to the British High Commissioners' office and inquired about passage to America. There, Mr. Hardy asked him if he was a government servant.

"No, sir," he replied, "I am God's servant."

"That will do," was Mr. Hardy's reply, and he gave Bakht Singh a passage to New York City.

Reuben Larsen of HCJB Radio met him when he arrived in New York City.[1] "You have come to America because of our prayers," he told Bakht Singh. "Many had been praying for someone to come who knows Hindi." The very first day there he recorded a radio message in Hindi for HCJB Radio. In the following days, Bakht Singh recorded thirty messages in Hindi and Urdu to be broadcast, one for each day, to Indian listeners in Latin America.

Bakht Singh visited various places throughout the United States and Canada before heading to Toronto to speak at the InterVarsity Student Missionary Convention. However, just before the convention he slipped on an icy sidewalk and fractured his elbow. When the doctors took an x-ray of his arm, they informed him that the fracture was so bad they would have to open up his arm and reset all the bones. It would take a month for his arm to heal, and he should not consider speaking at the convention.

Even though he was in excruciating pain, Bakht Singh decided to postpone the operation until after he had given the main message of the convention. According to those who where there that day, Bakht Singh gave a powerful message, "Counting the Cost of Serving Christ," based on Luke 14. A student asked Bakht Singh, "If you are a man of God, why did God allow you to slip and break your arm?" Bakht Singh answered that he did not know all the reasons, but he had been in so much pain from the broken arm he could not sleep, so he had spent the time praying for all the young people at the convention.

The Lord used Bakht Singh in a mighty way at that first Urbana Convention. Jim Elliot, Ralph Winter, and David Howard were among the nearly six hundred participants there that year, and about half of all the students who attended the conference went to the mission field.[2]

United States

Bakht Singh visited the United States several times after that first visit. Dr. Bob Finley of International Students, Inc., invited him to speak at the Indigenous Mission's Institute held in Washington DC in the summer of 1969. He wanted to help international students get a vision of establishing New Testament churches in their countries. Bakht Singh wrote of the conference.

> About seventy Christian leaders and students from twenty countries now studying or on business in the U. S. attended the sessions regularly. Besides the regular sessions during the day, there were special meetings every evening open to the public. . . . We were very much conscious of God's presence with us in every gathering. There has been daily, an increasing number of genuine enquiries from believers hailing from the United States and from other countries, about the establishing of indigenous churches in their respective countries. On Sunday, we had worship service. . . . There were believers from India, Philippines, Sudan, Ghana, Hong Kong, U. K., Japan, Singapore, Liberia, Sierra

Leone, Afghanistan, China, Thailand, Taiwan, Guyana, and Guatemala. The worship meeting was followed by an Indian-style love-feast of rice, curry, and vegetables. This gave us opportunity to have fellowship with one another very intimately. . . . We were convinced that the Lord would have us pray with a greater burden for the establishing of His living churches in various parts of the world.[3]

During his visit to the United States in 1969, Bakht Singh visited me in Syracuse, New York, to see our ministry to international students at Syracuse University. He was thrilled to see the unprecedented opportunity of reaching students from around the world. He asked me what was being done with those students who came to know Christ through our ministry. I told him that they were being sent to various Bible preaching churches in and around Syracuse University.

He thought for a while and then said, "Our responsibility is not only to see that men and women come to know the Lord Jesus Christ, but also to disciple them and to teach them about the body of Christ—the church." He said it was important to give these students the concept of the New Testament Church so that when they go back home, they can apply these principles in their own cultural backgrounds and thus increase the body of Christ in other parts of the world. He encouraged me to start a house church in order to disciple and equip the newly converted international students. I told him that I would pray about it with my wife, Indira, and we would do as the Lord led us.

On his next visit in the summer of 1970, he again emphasized the importance of starting a house church based on New Testament principles in Acts 2:42. On the Sunday while he was with us, we had a worship service and the Lord's Table that was attended by a large number of believers from in and around Syracuse. Then in September 1970, six of us met together in our living room. That was beginning of the local church ministry in the United States affiliated with the ministry of Bakht Singh. Since then, similar gatherings have started in various parts of the United States.

Bakht Singh also encouraged us to hold Holy Convocations for believers to come together for teaching and fellowship. Not having any experience in holding such a large gathering, I went into it with fear and trembling. In 1974, the first one was held for three days in Syracuse. Believers came from as far away as Pakistan and India as well as other places. Encouraged, we continued to hold the convocations each year. In 1977, they were moved to Cazenovia College in Cazenovia, New York, and stretched into nine days. The Lord used these convocations to give the vision for New Testament churches and the importance of the unity of the body of Christ to the hundreds who gathered there from many other countries.

France

After the Lord had given him the vision of the church based on New Testament principles, Bakht Singh's burden was to share the same vision with believers in various parts of the world. He wanted them not only to catch the same vision but also to help begin other churches or assemblies based on those principles.

While Bakht Singh was visiting Strasbourg in France, he met Earnest Verborne. Each time he visited Brother Verborne and his fellow believers, he would encouraged them to start a house church in the area. They named the church "Patmos," as a place of worship. Bakht Singh visited the church, where they worshiped together based on Acts 2:42. He then encouraged them to begin Holy

Convocations there. They held the first one in 1977 in a hotel in Sarcelles, France. These gatherings continued until 1984.

It was during the first French Holy Convocation in 1977 that Bakht Singh preached a message "The Return of God's Glory" that brought about a deep burden for prayer to those gathered. They began to pray for the body of Christ worldwide. They prayed every evening and sometimes all night. As a result, seven New Testament churches were established in France. Afterwards the ministry spread in other parts of Europe, particularly in Rumania.

New Caledonia

Brother Verborne felt strongly through his reading of Psalm 72:8, "from sea to sea," that the Lord was leading him to visit the new believers in New Caledonia who had been asking him to come. Ostracized by their tribe, they had to move to another part of the island and were facing many trials. The Lord used him there to reach many more people, some who walked an hour and a half to worship at the Lord's Table. Holy Convocations were held every year, and new gatherings sprang up throughout the area. The ministry of Bakht Singh is still bearing fruit in that area. At the time of this writing, there are eight local assemblies in France, four in New Caledonia, two in the Loyalty Islands and seven in the Archipelago of Vanuatu.[4]

Germany, Switzerland, and Other European Countries

Through the reading of Bakht Singh's testimonies and books as well as through the reports of missionaries from Europe working in India, many in Germany heard of Bakht Singh's ministry. He visited Germany several times and met Werner Tietze, who served as his translator there and in other European countries. For many years Werner sent out the letter, *Praise and Prayer*, from the Hebron Messenger. Some of Bakht Singh's books were translated and circulated in Germany. They inspired the young people who read them. German believers attended the Holy Convocations held in France, and as a result, the believers in France and Germany were united in fellowship.

Karl Frei of Winterthur, Switzerland, met Bakht Singh in Bangalore, India, while working there as an engineer. During his stay in India, he and Bakht Singh developed a strong friendship. When Frei moved backed to Switzerland, he was able to open many doors for Bakht Singh there and in Germany, Yugoslavia, France, and other eastern European countries. He translated Bakht Singh's books and distributed them and brought together the churches in many European countries for Holy Convocations.

United Kingdom, Denmark, and Holland

The church at Honor Oak in London was started when Austin-Sparks, a Baptist minister, received a fresh revelation of the body of Christ and left the Baptist Church. For many years Austin-Sparks and the saints with him prayed for India. In 1935, Fred Flack and Raymond Golsworthy were sent to India by the Honor Oak fellowship to do a new work. Lady Ogle from Honor Oak also traveled to India to help with the work. Through her, they met Bakht Singh. The friendship, which began over a cup of tea, lasted for decades, and Bakht Singh visited England many times.

In Denmark, Paul Madsen had a similar vision of the church. Bakht Singh spoke at the conference organized by him and his co-workers. People came from Finland, Norway, Sweden, Germany and all parts of Denmark. Even though Bakht Singh did not know the language, he reported, "Yet we felt perfectly one with them, and had a foretaste of heaven through their love and fellowship. We could exchange only a few broken words with each other, but still there was a consciousness of the flow of divine life in our midst. The number went up to more than four hundred and fifty towards the weekend. . ."[5]

In 1958, he visited Holland and met with a few believers, sharing his testimony and vision of the church. He spoke throughout the country on the subject of the "Return of God's Glory" and encouraged all to pray that God's glory would return to the church. About that visit Bakht Singh wrote:

> Brother Lugthart and about twenty other believers from Amsterdam were at the airport when I reached Amsterdam, and they gave me a very warm welcome in the Name of the Lord Jesus Christ. We had a sweet time of fellowship in a home where the saints, about twenty-five in number, had been gathering regularly since two years, for worship and breaking of bread. Amsterdam is the capital of Holland. It is a very needy city. Three fourths of the population refuse to be identified with any kind of religion. Too much prosperity has made the people spiritually blind. To see a group of believers in a city like this was like seeing an oasis in a desert.[6]

Australia

In 1956, Bakht Singh visited Sydney. He was invited by evangelical leaders to minister at different churches, over the radio, and at Christian rallies. The theme was revival, so he emphasized the importance of praying according to God's burden and will. There was a great expectancy for revival in many places. In one church, prayer meetings were held every morning for two years from six to eight o'clock.

In 1958 Bakht Singh was invited again by some evangelical ministers to teach and preach further on revival, and the work spread in the Sydney area and beyond.[7] In early 1959, a congregation was formed on the basis of Acts 2:42. Bakht Singh went back to Australia ten years later primarily to help those who were gathering together according to the New Testament church principles. He set apart elders in the first local assembly just outside of Sydney. Later, however, due to some doctrinal differences, most of the elders left that fellowship and joined Ernest and Kathleen Toussaint.

When Bakht Singh visited Australia again he wrote, "The Lord gave me a very precious and blessed time in Brisbane (Queensland, Australia), even though my stay there was for three days only. I could sense a great spiritual decline in that country. Yet in every place, the Lord has kept some witnesses who are giving the rightful place to the Lord Jesus Christ."[8]

Pakistan

Bakht Singh began his evangelistic ministry in Karachi in 1933. His burden then was to see people brought to Christ and begin to live in obedience to the will of God; he did not have any intention of setting up independent local churches. However, with the establishment of Jehovah-Shammah in Madras, he had a paradigm shift in his vision and mission, and he began emphasizing the importance of local churches.

Many who were converted at the Martinpur revival in 1937 began witnessing for Christ all across Punjab and Sindh and in other areas that are now part of Pakistan. Several believers from Punjab attended the Madras Holy Convocation in 1941 and returned with a fresh vision of the church. Dennis Clark, a missionary in the area, met with Bakht Singh at Jehovah-Shammah with the desire to work with him. Bakht Singh and the elders laid their hands on him as an expression of their oneness and identification with him in the work of the Lord.

Bakht Singh and his co-workers from Jehovah-Shammah traveled to Pakistan frequently, even after the partition of the country in 1947. During his visit in 1948, Dennis Clark and his co-workers arranged the first Holy Convocation in Lahore, which later grew to include over two thousand participants. The themes of these Holy Convocations often centered on the vision and functions of the New Testament church. Besides Bakht Singh, the Lord used men such as Daniel Smith, Raymond Golsworthy, A.J. Flack, Jordan Khan, and Dennis Clark to bring his message to the groups gathered at the convocations.

Dennis Clark established a publishing house in Lahore called Masih Ishait Khana (MIK) to help with literature for evangelism, discipleship, and spiritual growth in the ministry. It was a counterpart of Literature Service (GLS) of Bombay which was a great boost in the ministry of Bakht Singh in India.

In 1963, while visiting in Shantinagar, a predominantly Salvation Army village, some disgruntled Christians reported that Bakht Singh was an Indian Christian trying to create trouble in the village. Without any further enquiry into the matter, the Pakistan government deported him from the country he had loved and served.

Living in an Islamic fundamentalist country where missionaries and particularly Christians are treated worse than second-class citizens, many in the New Testament churches and assemblies became isolated and inward-looking. Internal strife and struggle, coupled with the lack of proper spiritual teaching and nourishment took its toll upon the believers. Though the political tensions between India and Pakistan prevented believers from these countries visiting each other, the Lord raised up the necessary help through other missionaries. Bakht Singh could no longer visit Pakistan, but his associates A.J. Flack, C.R. Golsworthy, Daniel Smith, Jordan Khan and others continued to visit the area. From 1993, I have also been helping the work in Pakistan.

Sri Lanka

God used different people to prepare the ground in Sri Lanka before a local assembly was established in 1949. An Indian evangelist, E.C. de Alwis, and his wife were converted to Christ. About that same time, one of the elders from Jehovah-Shammah received a transfer order to Sri Lanka. Even though the church at Jehovah-Shammah prayed for the order to be cancelled, George Rajaratnam had to move there. God needed him in Sri Lanka instead.

Mr. de Alwis had started a meeting in his home, and George Rajaratnam got in touch with him and the believers there. Through prayer and teaching he was able to heal a rift between two different groups, and the two groups began meeting together. When Bakht Singh visited Colombo later that year, he laid hands on four men to become elders, and the church became a true New Testament church.

Japan, the Philippines, Other Asian Countries

In his attitude and actions, Bakht Singh was a world-class Christian who had a global view of the body of Christ. He believed and taught that every believer in Christ, regardless of his or her nationality, language, caste, class, and color, is equally important and necessary. He traveled and preached Christ and shared the vision of the church with believers in many parts of the world without any personal vested interest. His vision was to see local churches on New Testament principles bring glory to Christ.

In 1947 he visited Japan and wrote this about his visit:

> The people of Japan as a nation are extremely superstitious and even believers are very easily led away by new and strange doctrines. Unless there is a living testimony to show forth the headship of the Lord Jesus Christ, one does not see much hope for Japan. When one sees the multitudes of Japanese being drawn away towards false cults, which provide them nothing but husks, one cannot but feel a strong burden for the Japanese nation.[9]

He traveled from Japan to the Philippines. He felt burdened to stay two weeks in the Philippines. For thirty years a group of Chinese Christians had been meeting in Manila. Even though the group was growing in number, much of their activity had been confined to the Chinese only. After Bakht Singh visited them he wrote, "For the past four years or so, there has been a new movement of the Holy Spirit and when I visited them this time I found a new burden of prayer. . . . It gives great joy to see that the hand of God has begun to move in their midst to do a new work in them and has given them a fresh heavenly vision of their responsibility towards people in other parts of Asia."[10]

He was greeted warmly in Taipei when he visited there. Many of the inhabitants of the island had gone through hardship due to Communist occupation in China in 1947. But this proved to be a blessing in disguise. Before, there were very few foreign missionaries on the island, but when all the missionaries were forced out of China, many of them moved to the island of Taiwan. About two hundred of them who had been with Watchman Nee settled there, and the Lord used them for the salvation of many. Taiwan is a beautiful island. Bakht Singh was impressed by the hard working people he met there. He wrote about Taiwan: "As a nation, the Chinese in Taiwan are very methodical and systematic in their way. This characteristic of theirs sometimes limits the free working of the Holy Spirit, and they need to be shaken occasionally to make them get out of their ruts. But then, I should say that, we all need such kind of shaking at times."[11]

Bakht Singh traveled to Singapore, Trinidad, and Indonesia and found Christians hungry for the Word of God and a number of young people going out in teams to take the gospel to all parts of the country. At the W.E.C. conference for South East Asian leaders, he challenged them to take the gospel to the uttermost parts of the world. Many accepted this challenge and dedicated their lives afresh to the Lord.

Africa

In August 1963, Bakht Singh spoke at the Keswick convention held in the capital of Malawi. People representing many denominations, countries, and backgrounds attended the conference. The oneness of the Body of Christ was the theme of the conference. From there Bakht Singh visited believers in the interior of Malawi and several countries in Africa.

He was always sensitive to God's leading as to what he should do. When he was in Nairobi a friend told him about the world famous Natural Zoo where people would come from all over the world just to see the animals walking about in their natural setting. Bakht Singh prayed and asked the Lord whether he should go to the zoo. The Lord advised him not to go because someone was going to come to see him. He told this to his friend who was very surprised and said, "You must come. It is a wonderful sight."

Bakht Singh answered, "No, I have not come to Nairobi to see monkeys and donkeys. I have come in the service of the Lord. I will go where he wants me to go and I will do what he wants me to do."

That same day a visitor came to see him. The visitor said, "Brother, I have traveled the whole night by bus from Mombasa, about five hundred miles, to see you. We have been praying that God would send you to us." Soon they arranged special meetings together, which the Lord blessed.

The Middle East

Following his visit to Africa in late 1963, Bakht Singh went to many countries in the Middle East. He was encouraged to see the way the Lord was using the believers in all places to influence others for Christ. He was refreshed by their fellowship and their hunger for the Word of God. He was able to see in person the greatness and largeness of God and his method of working among various countries, tribes, languages, and people groups to gather a people for Himself.

As Bakht Singh traveled around the world, God continued to provide guidance and provisions for him in unusual ways. While on his way to Zagreb, Yugoslavia, from Zurich, Switzerland, an announcement came over the loud speaker at the airport saying that the plane could not land at Zagreb due to bad weather there and would go directly to Belgrade, quite a long distance south of Zagreb. A special meeting had been arranged for Bakht Singh in Zagreb that evening, and he had no contacts in Belgrade, so he didn't know whether he should board the plane. He had only minutes to decide because the passengers were already boarding the plane.

After praying, he felt the Lord was telling him to board the plane. He obeyed and continued boarding, praying all the while that God would change the weather. A few minutes into the flight, the captain announced that the weather had cleared and they would land in Zagreb after all.

There are many stories like this that could be told about Bakht Singh—a place on a crowded train when all other seats were taken, or help from strangers to find accommodations in a hotel. Bakht Singh took the guidance of God very seriously and relied on the Lord's leading to make decisions about where to go and what to do. God used his faith to influence literally tens of thousands of people wherever the Lord led him.

Notes

1. Reuben Larsen was a co-founder of HCJB Radio in Ecuador, South America.
2. Author's interview with Dr. Christy Wilson, who was the missionary secretary of the convention that year.
3. *Hebron Messenger*, Editorial, September 14, 1969.
4. Verborne's letter to the author in 2002.
5. *Hebron Messenger*, Editorial, September 3, 1978.
6. *Hebron Messenger*, Editorial, June 20, 1965.
7. Information given by Ernest Toussaint to the author, 2002.
8. *Hebron Messenger*, Editorial, April 14, 1968.
9. *Hebron Messenger*, Editorial, December 19, 1965.
10. Ibid.
11. Hebron Messenger, Editorial, July 7, 1968.

Chapter 12

Spiritual Secrets of
Bakht Singh's Life and Ministry

For to me to live is Christ, and to die is gain.

Philippians 1:21

Crossing the Atlantic Ocean in 1928 on a ship bound for Canada, Bakht Singh had an encounter with the living Christ that completely revolutionized his life and thinking. The first words out of his mouth that night were "living Christ." He knew he had met Christ—not a person of the past, but someone who was alive and present. His life was changed from then on. He wanted to know more about this person of Christ and immediately began reading the Word of God. The subjective experience of his encounter with Christ was strengthened through his insatiable reading of the

Bible. The living Christ and his living Word became very precious to him.

His spiritual life, discipleship, evangelism, the church—all aspects of his life—were brought under the subjective experience of listening to the voice of Christ daily and the objective experience of accepting the Bible as the final authority for his faith and action. For his subjective experience to be valid and authentic, it had to be substantiated by the revealed Word of God.

He took God and His Word seriously, and his ability to wait upon God and hear His voice made his ministry and life unique. The following are some of the characteristics of his life.

He Listened For the Voice of the Lord

He said, "Once we learn the secret of hearing the voice of God, all our questions, no matter how difficult they are, are answered; and our problems, however complicated, are solved. The Lord does speak."[1]

Immediately after his conversion, Bakht Singh began reading through the Bible starting with Genesis. He noticed the words "God said" or "God spoke" several times on every page. He counted 558 times in just the first five books of the Bible. He thought to himself, "If God is speaking then I must listen," and he prayed that God would speak to him.

He wrote, "If you want to enjoy the grace of God and to understand His power in fullness, and to know the mind and the will of God everyday, then learn the secret of hearing His still small voice everyday and many times during the day. . . . God speaks to us through His Word. And if you believe in God you must listen when He speaks. He is not something abstract. He is a Person. We can know Him, hear Him, be led of Him and know Him more intimately than we know anybody else."[2]

Bakht Singh heard the voice of the Lord from the time of his conversion. He would normally hear this voice only in his spirit and not audibly, but there were a few occasions when he actually heard the voice of God with his physical ears. He made sure that the voice of God always corresponded with the written Word of God, because God does not contradict His Word.

There are three conditions that Bakht Singh thought were important to be able to hear God's voice: 1) repentance of sin and acknowledging Christ as Savior, 2) belief in the Word of God through divine light or revelation, and 3) a deep desire to know and to do the will of God. He had many examples from his life experiences of the Lord speaking to him and directing him.

He Depended Upon the Sovereignty of God

Bakht Singh believed with all his heart that God was sovereign and that no matter what happened to him, the Lord could turn his trials and tragedies into glorious triumphs. Even though he could not fully understand everything that took place in his life, he knew the Lord would use it to fulfill his purpose.

Bill Thompson, an English missionary who had worked with him in India, made this observation: "It was brother Bakht Singh's quiet rest in the absolute sovereignty of God that gave him his characteristic freedom from stress. On one occasion he was passing through Bombay on his way to London for a very important conference. In the taxi on the way to the airport in Bombay, he discovered that he had left his passport behind in Hyderabad. There was no way of getting it in less than a day and no hope of taking that flight without it. What would have thrown many into a panic left him calm and thankful for a God "'who worketh all things after the counsel of his own will.'"

On another occasion, Bakht Singh was to go to Bombay by air from Hyderabad. Before he left, he was delayed by so many people asking for prayer that his co-workers told him to hurry or he would miss his flight. Bakht Singh replied that if God wanted him to go to Bombay, he would take care of it. By the time he arrived at the airport, the plane had already left. He was not the least worried or concerned. He told his co-workers, "Don't worry. If the Lord wants me to go to Bombay, he will bring the plane back." Sure enough, a few minutes later the same plane returned to Hyderabad. Apparently, after the plane had taken off, one of the passengers, a wealthy woman, reported to the pilot that she had left a very costly diamond ring in the ladies room at the airport. She pleaded with the pilot to turn the plane around so she could look for her diamond ring. (Only in India might this happen.) The pilot consented, allowing Bakht Singh to catch the flight to Bombay.

There are many stories such as these that demonstrate Bakht Singh's total dependency on the sovereign will of God. George Verwer, an American missionary who worked closely with Bakht Singh, was asked about the impact Bakht Singh had made on his spiritual life. He said, "If I had to say one thing, I will say his emphasis on prayer and absolute confidence in God."[3]

He Accepted the Bible as the Word of God

He accepted the Bible as the infallible, inerrant, inspired Word of God from Genesis to Revelation. In this respect, he was a Biblical fundamentalist. He obeyed the Word of God implicitly. He placed a strong emphasis on the Scriptures as the constant, living source of instructions from God through the Holy Spirit.

All the songs that were sung in the meetings were based on the Scriptures. Scriptures were painted on the walls of the buildings or hung in the tents of the Holy Convocations. During the gospel campaigns in every place, the Bible Society sold out of Bibles. People had to go to the second-hand bookstores to buy Bibles. He always encouraged people to read and honor the Word of God.

Many who knew him remarked about his knowledge of the Scriptures. His insight into the Word of God and his photographic memory were legendary. George Verwer said, "His knowledge of the Word of God was a phenomenal thing. And his messages were so filled with Scriptures. He was a man of the Bible. The Bible was the Book, and he was like a walking concordance."

Dr. Martin Lloyd-Jones, the famed expositor and Bible teacher, and the Reverend Leith Samuel, one of the speakers at the Keswick convention, spent several hours with Bakht Singh. They asked him questions from the Bible, and Bakht Singh's answers challenged and surprised them. Then Martin Lloyd-Jones asked him how he got such insight into the Word of God. Bakht Singh told him by reading and meditating on the Word of God upon his knees until the Holy Spirit revealed the deeper things of God. Until he became ill, he read the Bible on his knees and meditated on it for hours at a time.

He Lived a Life of Faith

Bakht Singh had a child-like faith. He trusted the Lord for all of his personal and ministry needs throughout his life. He never sent out a letter nor made any public appeals to anyone, and he never allowed anyone to pray for his needs publicly, even in the assembly prayer meetings.

An elderly man at Jehovah-Shammah once noticed clothing needs of inmates and gave a prayer request during the Wednesday prayer meeting. Bakht Singh did not mention the need in the prayer, and after the meeting he rebuked the man for his lack of faith and belittling God.[4]

Daniel Smith put it well: "Bakht Singh had never been to the West to beg. His annual Holy Convocations in India require several thousands of US dollars, plus all the needs and cares of the work and workers. I have been as close as any to him, but I have never heard the slightest whisper about finance."[5]

Dr. Robert Bowman, co-founder of Far East Broadcasting Company, was surprised when Bakht Singh came to visit him during one of his visits to the United States. Bowman expected Bakht Singh to ask him for money for his ministry like many Christian workers from other countries did. Instead, Bakht Singh pressed a fifty dollar bill into Bowman's hand when they shook hands. Bakht Singh gave Dr. Bowman a gift for his ministry. Whenever people in the West asked him what they could do to help India, he would say, "The Lord is able to supply the need. What India needs is more of Christ and prayer for India."

Norman Grubb, the International Secretary of the Worldwide Evangelization Crusade, had this to say about his visit to the Holy Convocations in Hyderabad, "To us Westerners, the most striking part of the whole work with Bakht Singh are the Holy Convocations held annually at Hyderabad. . . . Thousands of people are massed together in close quarters and all fed by the Lord for a week with no appeals to man."[6]

As he prayed in faith and in private, the Lord laid upon the hearts of people to send in the money or whatever help was needed. For example, on one occasion Bakht Singh needed some money.

He prayed for an exact amount. While he was praying, another Indian believer was going to the bank to deposit a certain amount of money. The Lord spoke to that believer and told him to take the money to Bakht Singh instead. When the man arrived at his room, he found Bakht Singh on his knees praying. He handed Bakht Singh the envelope, and in it was the exact amount he had been praying for.

Another example happened in 1944 when there was a great shortage of rice as the elders were planning for a Holy Convocation in Madras. They needed to provide for about two thousand people daily, and the rationing authorities had not sanctioned enough rice to meet their needs. They did not know what to do. The people would need to eat. After they prayed, Bakht Singh had someone measure the amount of rice they had on hand and let him know the exact quantity. The man came back and said there were five extra bags. In those wartime days of severe rationing, they had to keep accurate accounts, and the account book showed no extra bags. Bakht Singh had the man measure again, and again there were five extra bags. They measured it three times. There was no doubt; by some mysterious means there were five more bags of rice than there should have been. They had rice left over at the end of the Holy Convocation.

During the 1968 Holy Convocation at Kalimpong, heavy rains fell for days. The residents of Kalimpong said they had never seen such a downpour in all the past years as far as they could remember. On top of that there was a strong earthquake that caused heavy landslides in the area. Many houses were swept away, and lives were lost. All the roads to Kalimpong were completely blocked. The many who came for the Holy Convocation were detained in Kalimpong, and there was no possibility of the roads and bridges being repaired for a long time to come. Bakht Singh and his co-workers had no idea when they would be able to get out, but the Lord gave them peace and assurance He would take care of them and that He had a greater purpose for them there.

He wrote:

> So in this unforeseen way, we had the great privilege of strengthening the believers who had to stay on for about an extra week or ten days. We were able to carry on our Bible studies morning and evening and at the same time take the gospel to the people in the town who had gone through much suffering due to the recent landslides. A very large number of tourists and visitors who were stranded in Kalimpong had nothing else to do but wander about the streets making enquiries from different people as to how and when they would be able to get away. This proved to be the best time to put forth the claims of the Lord Jesus Christ, who alone can give true comfort in every kind of distress.[7]

He goes on to tell about their rescue. Suddenly one day they began praying, "Lord, command the military and civil authorities to take us out of Kalimpong by helicopter." They felt the burden of the Holy Spirit to pray for this. Then Bakht Singh was given some unusual promises from Ezekiel 8:3: "And the Spirit lifted me up between the earth and the heaven." He took this as a clear indication that the Lord was going to answer their prayer and arrange an air-lift for them. A few days later the Lord gave him another verse from Ezekiel 12:3: "Prepare thy stuff for removing, and remove by day in their sight: and thou shalt remove from thy place to another place in their sight." They began to pack up their suitcases. The very next day helicopters airlifted more than half of their number out of the area.

The next morning, the rest of the group prepared to go to the helipad in the hope of getting airlifted out. Half way there, the jeep they were riding in ran out of petrol. Petrol was extremely scarce in the whole area; no one could buy even a small quantity. Bakht Singh wrote,

> Humanly speaking, it now looked impossible for us to reach the helipad. I prayed, reminding the Lord of the promise given to us from the book of Ezekiel. Just then, a believer and his wife who were living nearby came to our rescue with their jeep. Even though he had only a small quantity of petrol in his tank, by faith he made four or five trips to take our party and the luggage to the helipad. He was more and more surprised to see that each time he measured the amount of petrol in the tank with a stick, it always showed the same level! He was so impressed by this little incident that he went home joyfully and brought rice and curry and coffee and bread for the whole party.[8]

Several times during his travels, Bakht Singh went by faith, trusting in the Lord to find him a seat on a plane or train, and the Lord amazingly honored his faith. He tells of one time when he needed special sleeping berths on a train to accommodate a missionary and his wife who was recovering from an operation on her hip. The station master said that there was absolutely no way he would be able to give him the special berths. Bakht Singh replied, "God will provide." Just minutes before the train was to leave the station, the station master came back to tell Bakht Singh that there had been some kind of miracle. Someone had cancelled three sleeping berths, and they were now available.

He Was a Man of Prayer

People often found him on his knees, whether day or night. Those who worked closely with him remarked often that he was truly a man of prayer. Usually he began his day at four o'clock and prayed until six o'clock or so. He wanted to sense God's burden for the day rather than sharing only needs with God. Raymond Golsworthy, a co-worker of Bakht Singh for nearly sixty years, had this to say:

> In those days we lived in very close proximity to each other, and we got to know each other intimately. We lived together . . . had our meals together . . . traveled together on trains and buses, and often walked from village to village together. For much of the time, when we were in Madras, four or more of us shared a large "upper room" at Jehovah-Shammah, each in his own corner as it were. Often, when going to bed after a tiring day, we would see our brother wrap his Kashmir shawl around his shoulders and kneel down at his bedside for his "time of prayer," and no doubt, to go over the events of the day with his Master. If we looked up much later . . . we would usually see our brother in the same position, and with his lips still moving as he continued in his communion with God.[9]

Dennis Clark, another British missionary who worked with Bakht Singh in both India and Pakistan said, "Brother Bakht

Singh's prayers were earth-shaking. . . . In my whole life's experience, I have never heard the equal of Bakht Singh's prayers and the flow of prayer meetings wherever he went. . . . In Pakistan, late at night with his head under the mosquito net he would be praying. We had string beds on the mud-house roofs. It was very hot in late May or June. Before dawn he was already up, and I noticed his ankles moving against each other to ward off mosquitoes."[10]

Another missionary tells of going to meet Bakht Singh at 7:30 in the morning and finding the brothers already praying. He apologized for being late, thinking he had mistaken the time he was to be there. They told him he was not late but that they were just finishing the prayer meeting from the night before.

Many of his hosts and co-workers told stories of his prayer life: on his knees, praying late into the night and up again before anyone else to pray in the morning. It didn't matter if it was hot or cold. His days began with several hours of prayer, and throughout the day, every matter was brought before the Lord to seek his guidance. Before any meeting or conference, Bakht Singh would insist that everyone involved with the meeting or conference spend time, sometimes months, praying about it.

Dan Smith wrote in his brief biography of Bakht Singh, *A Prophet of God—Bakht Singh of India*: "No move is made and no journey undertaken without prayer. He never leaves a home without prayer, never receives or sends a visitor away without prayer, nor does this fervent and zealous spirit of prayer ever seem to be thrown off at any time or in any day. . . .

"His desires in prayer are very vigorous, flowing like a strong stream that cannot stay to creep into little holes or spend their energies in small crevices, Nothing is wasted by flowery language or trifles of the moment."[11]

There are many examples of how God answered his prayers. Once when Bakht Singh was holding a campaign in an open field with about seven thousand people in attendance, a swarm of insects suddenly came, as a storm. This is not unusual in South India. Such storms of insects come up like a thick wall, covering hands, feet, heads, and necks—even going into people's mouths and noses. No one could sit still to listen, and most of them began to leave. Bakht Singh asked them to please wait while they prayed. Bakht Singh prayed, "Lord in thy name we rebuke these insects which the devil has brought to disturb our meeting." Soon the insects fled away, and they were able to continue the meeting.

He was a Man of Simplicity and Humility

Bakht Singh was an unassuming man who took God, but not himself, seriously. He worked among the poor and needy, sitting and eating with them. He was accessible to anyone. He was never too busy or too big to meet those who came to him. I once shared a room with him at the Madras Holy Convocation in 1974. About three o'clock in the early morning, the village folks who were returning home after attending the Holy Convocation would come by to wake him up. He would get up, kneel down with them and pray, and then send them away and go back to sleep. About a half an hour later, while he was again sleeping soundly and snoring, another batch would come and shake him by the feet until he woke up. Once again, he would get up quietly and pray with them, and then send them on their way. This continued every thirty minutes or so. When the next batch came, I got up and told them not to wake him and suggested that somebody else could pray with them. But while I was talking, Bakht Singh woke up and said to me, "Please do not hinder them. Let me pray with them before they go." When I said to him that these people were disturbing him from his sleep, his answer was, "This is the little we can do for our fellow saints."

He Was Loving, Caring, and Hospitable

He was a spiritual father to tens of thousands both in India and abroad. He expressed his love by caring and being hospitable to the needs of others. Even though thousands attended his meetings, his piercing eyes would often detect those who were absent and enquire later why they were not at the meeting. He would be at their bedside, in their home, or in the hospital to pray and comfort the ones who were sick. He wanted to serve others, and he personally made sure that all guests were well taken care of.

Notes

1. Bakht Singh, *The Voice of the Lord*, (Bombay, India: Gospel Literature Service, 1970), p. 26.

2. Ibid., p.11.

3. George Verwer, founder of Operation Mobilization.

4. Martin Sathyanathan, *From Idols to the Service of the Living God*, (Andhra Pradesh, India: Salem Prayer House, 1993), p. 23.

5. Daniel Smith, *Bakht Singh of India: a Prophet of God* (Charlottesville, VA: Christian Aid Mission), p. 24.

6. Norman Grubb, *Once Caught, No Escape* (Fort Washington, PA: Christian Literature Crusade, 1970), p. 151–152.

7. *Hebron Messenger*, Editorial, November 10, 1968.

8. Ibid.

9. Raymond Golsworthy, "A Tribute to Brother Bakht Singh: He Taught Us to Pray," *Hebron Messenger* (Special Edition) September 17, 2000.

10. From Dennis Clark's letter, 1988.

11. Smith, p. 85–86.

Chapter 13

Bakht Singh's Vision for the Church

*By the grace God has given me, I laid a foundation as
an expert builder, and someone else is building on it.
But each one should be careful how he builds.*

1 Corinthians 3:10

Bakht Singh's concept of the church was the result of his personal experience with Christ. He believed that Christ should be magnified and glorified through the church and that the church was to show Christ's love, life, liberty, and light to the world. He searched the Scriptures, asking the Lord to show him the truth for the church, and after waiting on God in prayer and fasting, he received a fresh vision of the church. Some of the salient features of the New Testament Church that Bakht Singh preached and practiced are outlined in this chapter.

171

The Concept of the Church

The church is a spiritual community of the redeemed people of God of all classes and castes and nationalities. As the body of Christ, it includes all believers of Jesus Christ under the headship of the living Christ. It is not national or international but spiritual in nature.

The English word "church" is translated from the Greek word "ecclesia," which means "called out." The church includes only those who receive the Lord Jesus Christ as their Savior and Lord. They are called out of the world by Christ and united into His body, the church. According to Acts 2:47, the Lord added souls daily to the church, not to a building but to a group of people who believed in the Lord Jesus and received his Spirit. God's wisdom will be revealed through the church—not through angelic beings but through the redeemed people of God (Ephesians 3:9–11).

Bakht Singh identified two major aspects of the church: one local or visible and the other universal or invisible. True believers are already united in the "one body" when they are regenerated by the Holy Spirit, according to 1 Corinthians 12:12–13: "The body is a unit, though it is made up of many parts; and though all its parts are many, they form one body. So it is with Christ. For we were all baptized by one Spirit into one body—whether Jews or Greeks, slave or free—and we were all given the one Spirit to drink." The church is, therefore, one, and all believers throughout the world and throughout the ages belong to each other.

As mentioned in chapter 10, the local church constitutes a group of believers assembling together under the headship of Christ. The church is not an organization or an institution but a living organism where the redeemed people of God are spiritually united with Christ as the head. Every local church should be led by elders, as seen in the book of Acts: "The provision or appointment of elders in all the churches appears vital to their constitution as a local church."[1]

Bakht Singh preached and practiced the priesthood of all believers and rejected ecclesiastical order on the basis of the Word of God as in 1 Peter 2:9: "But you are a chosen people, a royal priesthood, a holy nation, a people belonging to God, that you may declare the praises of him who called you out of darkness into his wonderful light."

He emphasized the functions of the church, based on Acts 2:41–47, which include baptism of new believers, teaching the Word of God, fellowship, and the Lord's Table, as well as prayers and worship on a weekly basis, at least. He taught and practiced that the church as a corporate body must be actively involved in evangelism, discipleship, planting of new living assemblies, and ministering to the needs of both believers and non-believers.

Baptism: Baptism must follow repentance and faith in the Lord Jesus Christ; it cannot precede them in any form. Water baptism is not to be made a means of salvation or a method of joining the church. "Those who accepted his message were baptized, and about three thousand were added to their number that day" (Acts 2:41).

Laying on of hands: Bakht Singh practiced the laying on of hands following baptism. Some Christians view this practice as unnecessary, controversial, and divisive. Bakht Singh's teaching is stated in the following excerpt from his writings:

> We saw also from the Word of God that "laying on of hands" was associated with baptism, usually after, [but] sometimes before. . . . By looking at all the references from Genesis to Revelation, we concluded that this was

done in all cases to express the existence of a relationship. It might be the relationship of father and son, Moses and his successor, the congregation and those set apart to serve them, the offerer and the sacrifice he brought, the Lord and the least of His Kingdom (the little children) or the Church or its individual members. We concluded that when the church "laid hands" upon those who had testified to their union with Christ in baptism, it was to express and to declare that all such are related to them in the "one body." . . .

We have been accused of teaching that those on whom hands have not been laid were not in the body of Christ, which of course is quite false. Others have thought that it was by this means that believers were reckoned to belong to us or not. Others have thought that the laying of hands might be considered as the way to receive the Holy Spirit. Nothing of the kind! All believers belong to us and we to them; there is only one Body. All that we do must express this and be true to that fact.[2]

Bakht Singh believed that in this fallen world where the body of Christ is divided by so many natural and human factors, the laying on of hands could be a beautiful symbolic expression of our relationship and oneness in the body of Christ. This is especially true in a country such as India where believers range from high-caste to outcaste, and they avoid each other like the plague. Bakht Singh sought to break down those barriers by helping believers understand their unity and equality in Christ, both men and women, regardless of their place in society. He wanted the church to reflect this.

The Lord's Table: Bakht Singh believed in and practiced the weekly observance of the Lord's Table. (1 Corinthians 11:25, "Do this in remembrance of me.") The Table was open to all believers regardless of their nationality, color, caste, and status, but all believers were advised to partake of it in a worthy manner. It was another expression of the church as one body. Following the Lord's Table one of the brethren would lead in intercessory prayer, reminding everyone that the broken pieces of bread which remained spoke of the members of the body worldwide.

Praying for the sick: Bakht Singh believed in the gifts and the ministry of the Holy Spirit. He also believed in praying for the sick. "Is any one of you sick? He should call the elders of the church to pray over him and anoint him with oil in the name of the Lord. And the prayer offered in faith will make the sick person well; the Lord will raise him up. If he has sinned, he will be forgiven" (James 5:14–15).

After anointing the sick with oil, Bakht Singh would lay his hands on them and pray for their healing. In many cases the Lord honored his prayer in remarkable ways for those suffering from sickness as well as from demon possession. Bakht Singh did not want attention drawn to himself or to the healing. He did not want them publicized or misunderstood as a way into the Kingdom of God or proof of God's working. He believed that the strongest and clearest evidence of a movement of God was transformed lives.

Choosing Speakers: Bakht Singh did not believe in pre-arranged ministry. He did not plan or arrange before hand who should speak or preach at any particular meeting. He wanted the Lord to direct someone with a message for the people through the Holy Spirit.

He would plan ahead only if a speaker were invited for a series of meetings.

From the beginning he taught that all had the responsibility toward God and the people to be burdened and exercised about the message. Each one was to individually seek the Lord's guidance for the message. He felt that a "one-man ministry" was wrong but also that an "any-man ministry" was just as wrong. Therefore, those responsible for the meeting met together beforehand for prayer and to inquire of each other as to who had a word from the Lord.

The Body life: Bakht Singh believed that Christ is the head of the church and in charge of all the affairs of the local church. Everything should be done for the edification of individual and collective members of the body and the extension of the kingdom. Thus, all believers, especially those in leadership, should seek to be led by the Holy Spirit in all things. He taught and encouraged every believer to do his or her part for the smooth functioning of the body of Christ, based on Romans 12 and 14 and 1 Corinthians 12.

There was no distinction made between full-time or self-supporting workers and other believers. All were equal before God. One of the great secrets of Bakht Singh's expansion of the local churches throughout India was the corporate functioning of believers employed in secular jobs working along side full-time workers. All gave themselves to the work of the Great Commission to build the church.

Provision of Shepherds: As the assemblies began to multiply, the need for shepherds became a pressing necessity. Every local church needed shepherds to live among them and be one of them to help them to maturity. The Lord answered this need in two ways: many small churches came into being through the ministry and care of local brothers who became the shepherds for those assemblies. But in other places where there was no one to take up that role, Bakht Singh would ask the Lord to call and set apart those who could go for a period of time to meet the needs of those churches.

God's Servants or Full-time Workers

Those who felt called of God to serve the Lord full-time, both men and women, came trusting the Lord with no promise of salaries or human security. They lived together, suffered together, and experienced the Lord together. The miracle was that in spite of their different backgrounds they continued together in harmony, for the most part.

The primary purpose of God's servants was to build up and help the local believers become mature so local leadership could be chosen from among them to continue the work. Just as the Apostle Paul sent Timothy, Titus, and others for a period of time, Bakht Singh, too, practiced the same principle by sending God's servants wherever their help and ministry were needed. The usual practice was that those men were transferred from assembly to assembly within three to four years with a few exceptions. Every year following the Holy Convocation in Hebron, he would hold two days of workers' meetings. During the meetings, he would pray and seek the Lord's mind about the transfers. Then at the close of the meetings, he would mention the names of the brethren and the places of their transfers in his prayer. That was how the brothers were informed as to where and when they were transferred. Most complied except for a few rare cases when someone would ask for permission to stay at a post because of children's education or circumstances such as that.

From the late seventies onwards, however, Bakht Singh became extremely busy with the work worldwide and did not have sufficient time to insist on the transferring of God's servants periodically. As a result, some of God's servants stayed on too long and became like denominational pastors, which adversely affected the work, leading to conflicts between the local believers and God's servants. This caused the break-up of some assemblies and even to some court cases.

Bakht Singh taught believers to contribute generously and joyfully to the work of the Lord. Those who served as God's servants were supported by the local church in which they served. They learned to live simply and were satisfied with what the Lord gave them. There was no central fund or distributing center for the support of the Lord's servants.

The Training of Workers

Bakht Singh did not believe in any formal Bible school or seminary training as a prerequisite for work or ministry of the Lord. He decided to follow the example of Christ who gathered his disciples together before he sent them out. They learned by being with him for a period of time before he sent them out to preach what they had been taught. This was also the way the apostles of the early church prepared for their ministry and the way they prepared younger fellow workers.

Thus Bakht Singh gathered his followers together from time to time for Bible study and instruction, usually for three weeks. They spent time together in Bible study and prayer and had a time of spiritual refreshment.

Indigenization of the New Testament Principles in the Local Churches

Bakht Singh wanted the church to be an expression of the oneness and equality of all believers. He was not after a national, Indian, Chinese, or American church but one universal church. Indigenization simply meant applying the New Testament principles of the church within the cultural background of the people without compromising the Word of God. It also meant self-supporting, self-governing, and self-propagating churches under the headship of Christ.

Every local church should be inclusive and open to all believers who wish to be a part of it. Many of the churches established by Western missionaries were foreign to the people of India because they brought Western culture to India along with Christ. Sadhu Sundar Singh once said, "Indians do need the water of life, but not in a European cup. They should sit down on the floor in church: they should take off their shoes instead of their turbans. Indian music should be sung. Long informal addresses should take the place of sermons."[3]

Years later, God used Bakht Singh to fulfill the expressed desire of Sadhu Sunder Singh.[4] George Verwer, who worked closely with Bakht Singh in Hebron, Hyderabad, made the following observation about his ministry.

> Bakht Singh's ministry is a phenomenal example of contextualization in its earliest days without compromising the Word of God. He liked the simple old gospel but he served it in a simple Indian cup. People sitting on the mats on the floor with their chappals or shoes off, singing authentically Indian music with Indian instruments. His messages were long, simple,

filled with Scriptures and with appropriate witnessing stories and explanation. He was humorous and a man of great charisma. Following the worship service on Sundays people sat on the mats on the floor and had meals together—love-feasts, fellowshipping with one another.[5]

Worship

One of the unique aspects of Bakht Singh's ministry was to teach and to practice Biblical worship. The believers, both male and female, were encouraged to worship the Lord audibly one by one because Bakht Singh believed, on the basis of Scripture, worship is the spiritual birthright of every believer. Specific time was set apart for pure worship where the saints were encouraged to magnify and glorify the Lord through praise and thanksgiving, sometimes lasting over an hour or more.

Usually Sunday morning service began with an opening prayer by one of the leading brethren, followed by worship or devotional songs that were most often composed by those in the congregation in the local languages accompanied by Indian musical instruments. Then an elder or a leading brother would give a brief exhortation focusing on Christ. Kneeling down one by one, the believers would pour out their praise and thanksgiving. Bakht Singh had discovered that one of the secrets of developing the life of Christ in the soul and spirit of a believer was through Spirit-led, individual worship in a corporate setting.

Place of Worship

From the very beginning, the assemblies met together for worship and weekly activities in rented houses. Bakht Singh believed that they should not spend too much money on physical buildings for the service of the Lord. The Lord does not live in temples made with hands; instead redeemed people are the temple of the Lord. Whenever the houses became too small for the gathering, they built tent-like halls or pandals for the gatherings. At times he had bamboo sheds built. Perhaps he wanted to show a contrast to the pretentious and expensive stone buildings of Western design.

He sat the people on floor mats, native style, and not on Western-style benches; he had the people compose their own hymns and psalms and set them to native music; he brought in Indian instruments of music to lead congregational singing; he kept meetings going for long hours at a time compared to infamous Western one-hour meetings. Bakht Singh wanted them to give and not beg and to seek guidance about every matter directly from the Lord instead of slavishly following the orders of the missionary.[6]

Every local church took the initiative to construct an appropriate facility within their means. Bakht Singh believed that every church was autonomous and self-supporting. He did not believe in centralized control or federation of churches. He believed in spiritual unity and fellowship of all scattered assemblies in India and throughout the world.

Chosen Brethren or Elders

In 1982, Bakht Singh had to undergo surgery for an enlarged prostate gland. Parkinson's disease, a debilitating condition, had already weakened him. It became clear to him that he would need help in the ministry. In December of that year, he requested that a few join him to "wait on the Lord to know His mind regarding the future of the ministry, particularly that of the hundreds of assemblies in Andhra Pradesh and other places." The following brothers were chosen: Brother C.E. Dasan of Hebron, Hyderabad; Brother K. Phillip of Jehovah-Shammah, Madras; Brother S. Martin of Waltair; Brother Lazar Sen of Ahmedabad; Brother Amrit Raj of Bangalore; and myself, Brother T. E. Koshy of Syracuse, New York, USA.

About this meeting, Bakht Singh wrote in the March issue of the Hebron Messenger: "After much prayer and fasting, we have found six brothers to assist me in different ministries. They will shoulder various responsibilities in the work of the Lord worldwide as the Lord leads."

Seeking the Lord's Will

One of the evangelical leaders of India once said that in the nineteenth century the Lord raised up men such as Hudson Taylor and George Muller to teach the Church the importance of doing God's work in faith. And in the twentieth century, the Lord raised up Bakht Singh to teach the body of Christ to seek and do the will of God corporately.

From the beginning, he was a team player. Dr. Angus Kinnear, a British medical missionary who worked with Bakht Singh from 1940 on, said that the most remarkable thing about the work associated with Bakht Singh was that before they made any important decision whether in relation to the speaker, place, or whatever it may be, Bakht Singh would meet with his co-workers to pray and seek the mind of Christ. Without unanimity they would not act.[7]

Rajamani recalls how on one occasion Bakht Singh was invited to Colombo and had bought his ticket to leave the next day. As they prayed with him that evening, however, one of them did not think he should go. Bakht Singh cancelled the ticket and delayed his travel until all were united in heart. When he eventually arrived in Ceylon, now Sri Lanka, events proved beyond a shadow of a doubt that the delay was God's timing.

George Verwer was amused and surprised by the practice of selecting speakers at the last minute before the meetings.

> To me, as a Westerner so well organized, we have to know months in advance who is going to speak. In contrast to that, Bakht Singh would wait upon God and often even he did not know who was going to minister in the evening meeting until just before the meeting. Just before the meeting he would call a group of brothers for prayer and then he would ask me if I had a message.[8]

In 1959, during his visit to the United Stated, he was staying with a friend. He needed haircut, so he prayed and asked the Lord whether he should go that day to the barber. He felt restrained from going that day, but a few days later he felt that he should go for his haircut. While he was getting the haircut, he shared his testimony with the barber Bruce, who was alone. By the time the haircut was over, Bruce was ready to kneel down there in the barbershop with Bakht Singh to receive Christ as his Savior. When Bakht Singh asked for the price of the haircut, Bruce said that he had received a priceless blessing from Bakht Singh and therefore there was no charge for his haircut. Bakht Singh said that because he had asked the Lord for the right time to go for his haircut, the Lord had prepared Bruce to be all alone in his shop.

Once I asked him why he sought God's will for the obvious things. He answer was to never take anything for granted.

See the appendix for Bakht Singh's guidelines to finding God's will.

Love-feasts

One of the salient features of the assemblies was the love-feast following the Sunday worship service. Some assemblies would prepare all the food themselves for all those who would come. In others, the believers were encouraged to bring dishes for themselves and to pass around for others. The main purpose was to provide an opportunity for believers to get together and have fellowship with one another over a meal. These meals helped to break down barriers based on color, language, caste, or any other man-made divisions, and in a practical way, they demonstrated the acceptance of each other in Christ.

Holy Convocations

The Holy Convocations have been one of the hallmarks of Bakht Singh's work and ministry. For him, they expressed the unity of the body of Christ. They have done much to break down the walls of separation and build bridges of relationship among people of various castes, colors, and backgrounds. He based them on the Old Testament, particularly Leviticus 23:4 where God told Moses that they should celebrate the seven feast of Jehovah: "These are the feasts of the LORD, even holy convocations, which ye shall proclaim in their seasons" (KJV).

Evangelism, Gospel Raids, and Gospel Processions

At heart, Bakht Singh was an evangelist. From the time of his conversion, he began distributing tracts and witnessing to others about Christ. He did both personal and mass evangelism. He always carried tracts to distribute to whomever he might come in contact with. In order to evangelize people more effectively, Bakht Singh organized gospel campaigns, gospel processions, gospel raids, door-to-door visitation, and open-air and street evangelism.

Every place he went for meetings, Bakht Singh held gospel processions of tens of thousands of saints marching around the cities, towns, and villages, several abreast, stretching out for miles in length, singing, praising, glorifying God, and declaring his glory among the heathens and pagans. In the days of revival meetings, believers from different denominations and backgrounds marched together showing forth the oneness and unity of all believers regardless of their color, caste, denomination, or doctrine.

Relationship with Other Mission Organizations

Contrary to the notion of some of his critics that he was anti-foreign and anti-missionary, Bakht Singh's record shows otherwise. From the beginning of his work, he linked with men and women who shared in his vision and mission. He had an open heart toward God's servants whether they were nationals or foreigners. While some missionaries worked in harmony and in unity by identifying themselves with Bakht Singh and the assemblies from the beginning, he also linked with likeminded Western missions and missionaries. His close working relationship with WEC (World Evangelization Crusade) and Operation Mobilization is note worthy.

In the early 1950s, Norman Grubb, then international secretary of WEC, visited Bakht Singh at Hebron, Hyderabad. After spending a few days with him and his co-workers, he wrote the following:

> What impressed me most on my Asian visit was my eight days with Bakht Singh and his co-workers and congregations. Here was to me a sample of the coming

world-wide church of Christ, where every nation has its
own anointed men of God, its self-supporting and self
propagating churches, which in due course will begin to
send witnesses to all parts of the earth just as much as the
churches in the West sent their witnesses to other lands.
. . . We found such a oneness of the Spirit with them. . . .
The result has been an unbroken co-operation for about
twenty years. . . .[9]

In the mid 1960s, the Lord brought George Verwer and the
OM (Operation Mobilization) team and trucks to India to link up
with Bakht Singh's ministry. The "OMers" were young and inexpe-
rienced but enthusiastic and energetic, radical and idealistic, and
ready and eager to do extensive evangelism with Bakht Singh in
Andhra and other parts of India.

George Verwer and his team appreciated all that they were able
to learn during their time in India. Working with Bakht Singh and
his ministry trained and equipped them to be men and women of
God. George Verwer says of this time,

Here we were, we did not look perhaps as shiny as we
should, people traveling all around in these old trucks.
. . . We used to set up book exhibitions at the Holy
Convocations, not just the Bibles and Hebron books
. . . but he would let us bring in many other books,
written by various authors on various subjects; he was
very open minded, more than some people thought. He
was more broad-minded, than some of his co-workers
and associates.[10]

The Lord enabled Bakht Singh and his co-workers to imple-
ment various aspects of the New Testament Church within the

cultural backgrounds of the people of God in India. He tried his best to do all things in obedience to His will in the light of the Word of God. Of course, being human he too had his frailties, and he was the first to admit it because he was a man of humility. He also demonstrated that when we do God's work in God's way, we will have the abundance of God's resources to carry out His purposes. We can learn a great deal from the life and ministry of Bakht Singh in understanding the true meaning and the purpose of the Church in the world today.

Notes

1. Bakht Singh, *Write the Vision*, (unpublished papers, 1966).
2. Ibid.
3. V. K. Bawa, *Christianity Is Indian: The Emergence of an Indigenous Community*, ed. Roger E. Hedlund, (Delhi, India: ISPCK for MIIS, 2000) p. 130–34.
4. In is interesting that Bakht Singh came to know Christ in December 1929, the same year Sadhu Sunder Singh disappeared. No one seems to know how he died.
5. Author's interview with George Verwer, 1991.
6. Bakht Singh, *Hebron Messenger*, (Special Edition, Part II, for Silver Jubilee of Jehovah-Shammah, Madras, July 24, 1966) p. 7.
7. Author's interview with Dr. Angus I. Kinnear on April 20, 1991, London, England.
8. Author's interview with George Verwer in 1991.
9. World Conquest, July–August 1956.
10. Author's interview with George Verwer in 1965.

Chapter 14

Man of God: Feet of Clay

But we have this treasure in jars of clay to
show that this all-surpassing power is from
God and not from us.

2 Corinthians 4:7

When Bakht Singh was young, he had a peacock tattooed on the wrist of his left hand. It remained on his wrist even after his conversion, for he could not erase it. Whenever people asked him about it, he said that the peacock had legendary colorful feathers, which were the envy of other birds. Whenever the peacock danced, showing all of its beautiful and colorful feathers, it would feel proud of its enviable beauty, but when the peacock looked at its feet, which were so ugly, the bird would feel humbled and would feel like hiding them. This is a true picture of Bakht Singh.

Although the Lord had blessed him with a legendary photographic memory and many other gifts, he often felt humbled realizing his own human limitations. On the one hand, he was an expression of God's grace and glory; while at the same time, he humbly knew he was also a man with feet of clay. He often said he was what he was because of the sheer grace of God and was thus in no way better than anybody else.

As a young man, I was invited to pray with Bakht Singh along with other brethren who were close to him. During such prayer times, Bakht Singh would begin by confessing his sins, even weeping while praying. I often wondered and was puzzled because everyone looked up to him as a man of God and as a saintly man. But Bakht Singh realized his own limitations and frailties before God.

He was different in private from in public. In private he was a man of great wit and humor. He would tell stories during times when we were gathered together for a meal or fellowship, laughing at his own jokes, like the time when he first went to England in 1926. It was very cold and he slept on top of the bedspread because people in India usually sleep that way. He shivered all night in the cold, not finding any blankets to cover himself. In the morning his landlady asked him if he had had a good sleep. "No," he replied, "it was too cold to sleep well." Then the lady showed him the blankets under the bedspread and explained how one should sleep *under* the blankets on the bed.

He told simple stories to the people in the villages, but he was outspoken, firm, and stern to the religious leaders, especially denominational leaders and missionaries. Thus some judged him to be arrogant and proud with a holier-than-thou attitude. He loved and cared for all whether they were Christians or non-Christians, but at the same time, he did not feel free to work closely with certain segments of the Christian community because he did not think they followed the Word of God. He was highly critical of the way they often misled people by not telling the whole truth of the gospel. For example, he was a very outspoken critic of modern and liberal missionaries as well as national workers who refused to emphasize that Jesus Christ is the only Savior.

As people were converted through his ministry, they often left the churches established by foreign missionaries and their Indian counterparts and joined the assemblies established by Bakht Singh's ministry. Naturally, many strongly criticized him, calling him a "sheep stealer." They punished the innocent people, formerly employees and members of their churches, who left to join the assemblies. Many lost jobs they held in missionary institutions such as schools, colleges, hospitals, and orphanages.

Some disliked Bakht Singh simply because he was not ordained by any denomination nor had any Bible school training. Therefore, everything he did was contrary to their ecclesiastical and denominational background.

He was also accused of being exclusive and refusing to work with other Christian groups. This was not true. He participated and spoke at numerous conferences, groups, and churches both in India and abroad. However, when he received an invitation from India or abroad, he sought the will of God as to whether he should attend and then waited to be led by the Lord. He was extremely busy taking care of the needs of the ever multiplying and growing local churches. Therefore, very often he had to say no to the invitations that came from other groups or organizations.

Unfortunately, people who did not know him closely thought that he was exclusive, thinking that only those local churches established by him were the true church. No doubt in the early days he was very outspoken and highly critical of liberal denominations, and some might have thought that he believed the assemblies were the only true church; in fact he was trying to say that salvation was only through Jesus Christ and not through any other means.

There was criticism of him within his own ministry as well. Some were concerned with the leaders that were chosen who turned out to be self-seeking and who caused havoc in the churches. Even when days of intense prayer went into the decision of who should be in leadership, Bakht Singh made a different decision for the sake of peace and unity. Some were concerned that even with a phenomenal knowledge of the Bible, he neglected to get some of the deep problems solved. But often how one interprets and applies Biblical principles to resolve conflict can differ and be misunderstood.

When Bakht Singh first began using the term "God servants," he never thought it would end up as a special class of leaders in the ministry. From his writings, preaching, and teachings, we see that Bakht Singh was opposed to God servants functioning as the pastor in any local church. But unfortunately, in a number of cases, God's servants failed to see this as a problem. Others criticized him for allowing these "servants" to stay on in some assemblies longer than they should and to cause the mistaken concept of the role and position of the servant of God to develop.

His spirit of generosity and humility was in marked contrast to some of his fellow-workers but at times could border on the naïve when it came to dealing with the influence of less broad-minded men, including co-workers. This caused irreparable damage in his working relationship with some of his co-workers and the ministry as a whole. Many denominations go to the extreme of doing everything based on their constitutions and laws; Bakht Singh seemed to have gone to the other extreme of not paying much attention to legal requirements. Unfortunately, that affected the overall work. Bakht Singh thought that his fellow believers were as sincere as he was and that they would be guided by the Lord. Therefore, he paid very little attention to legal requirements and infrastructure, to the detriment of some aspects of the ministry.

Those on the inside as well as the outside of the ministry often leveled charges of despotism against him. He was a no-nonsense leader. He burned with zeal for the Lord and always kept the Lord's interests and His kingdom first. This was reflected in his attitude and actions toward others and was often misunderstood. A casual observer might have thought Bakht Singh was authoritarian, but those who worked with him knew differently. Geoff Abbiss, a WEC missionary who, along with his wife, worked closely with Bakht Singh for about twenty years in Hebron, had this to say, "I know that he has been accused of authoritarianism, if not dictatorialism—others may have found him so, as they interpreted things, but that was not our experience."[1]

George Verwer observed of Bakht Singh: "He was a gifted leader. He was accused of being authoritarian. But how is one going to get anything done in a place like India, with all those different backgrounds, different castes, poor people, rich people, doctors, uneducated—how is he going to get things done if someone does not take some leadership. Bakht Singh knew how to lead people."[2]

The other factor to consider in regard to the charge of being authoritarian is that of culture. Many believers look up to their spiritual leader like a "Guru." In this case, many would come to Bakht Singh to ask him to pray to find out God's will for them for everything from marriage to finding a job. They did this not only with Bakht Singh but also with other spiritual leaders. But with Bakht Singh, because of his spiritual leadership and fatherly image, such respect was given to him. Thus this aspect is more cultural than spiritual.

The great lesson we learn from all this is that, while he was a man of God, he was also a man with feet of clay. Nevertheless, we can praise the Lord for this trophy of His grace who made himself available to the Lord and was used to establish hundreds of local churches.

Notes

1. From Geoff Abbiss' impression on Bakht Singh (from written notes to the author dated 2001).

2. Based on author's interview with George Verwer at his office in London, 1991.

Chapter 15

Conclusion

*Blessed are the dead who die in the Lord from
now on. . . . They will rest from their labor, for
their deeds will follow them.*

Revelation 14:13

Bakht Singh was best known in India as a planter of New
Testament churches within the culture and linguistic background
of the people. In this respect he could be called the father of modern
indigenous churches. He began his ministry at a critical period of
India's political history when the great transition from the British
Raj to an independent nation was at its peak. What was true with
the foreign rulers was also true of the foreign missionaries.

Bakht Singh realized that New Testament principles could be
applied without compromise to any cultural or national background.

People could identify with the New Testament churches or assembly without feeling that they were imported from another country or culture.

He also emphasized the all-inclusive nature of the local churches. He believed that every local church should be open to all believers in Christ, regardless of their caste, color, language, nationality, or position. One of the social ills and curses of India has been the caste system, where low-caste people are treated as the scum of the earth. As mentioned in other chapters, this was practiced even among Christians. From the beginning, Bakht Singh preached against this practice from the Word of God and practically demonstrated the fact that we are all one in Christ by his identification with people of all castes and classes. He instituted the love-feasts, or common meal, following the weekly meetings to break down the caste system in a practical way. Here one could find believers from different caste backgrounds in harmony, as members of the same spiritual family—sitting together, eating together, serving the Lord together, and even drinking from a common cup at communion.

Because of his love and care for people in all situations, he endeared himself to everyone who in turn responded with love and affection for him. He was a spiritual father to many who would come to him for prayer, counsel, and spiritual guidance. He denounced all the evil practices of traditions and cultures that encroached into areas of Christian marriage. In India, normally it is common practice for people to marry within their own caste, class, profession, language, state, and even color. Bakht Singh emphasized that people of God marry only another believer and according to God's will.

He made an impact at the international level by challenging and influencing believers to do "God's work in God's way." He was more concerned with the spiritual aspect of the church, which transcends all barriers. His desire was to see all nationalities, colors, classes, and castes of God's people gathered together to worship Him. He believed and taught that the church, the body of Christ, consisted of all believers worldwide.

Bakht Singh accepted the Bible as the Word of God from Genesis to Revelation and tried to apply biblical principles in every aspect of his individual or corporate life, whether big or small. Therefore, he did not believe in any policy or church constitution that was contrary to the Word of God. He denounced traditional and ecclesiastical practices that he felt were not completely founded upon the revealed Word of God.

Bakht Singh trusted God for every need, both personal and corporate. He encouraged his fellow workers and fellow believers to do the same. He demonstrated to everyone that if you do God's work according to His will, God will provide for your needs without having to publicly appeal for financial support from anyone. He also taught his fellow believers to give generously.

Through his life of faith and ministry, Bakht Singh showed forth the faithfulness and greatness of God. He loved Him and served Him faithfully for over sixty years and has left a spiritual legacy for us to follow.

Bakht Singh's Guidelines for Finding God's Will

Generally there are seven evidences by which we can make sure of God's perfect will:

1. The witness of the Holy Spirit with our spirit, as when God spoke to Samuel, "Arise, anoint him; for this is he." (1 Samuel 16:12).

2. The witness of the Word of God. We read in Psalm 119:105, "Thy word is a lamp unto my feet, and a light unto my path." It is for our safety to get God's will confirmed through some portion of God's Word, which we read during our morning devotional time. It is very profitable to read the Bible systematically and prayerfully as far

as possible upon our knees and seek God's guidance from the portion we read.

3. The registration given to fellow believers, co-workers, and God's servants. Daniel also prayed with his friends, (Daniel 2:17–19); then as they prayed together God revealed the secret to Daniel.

4. The inward peace in our hearts as we pray regarding some particular matter. "The work of righteousness shall be peace; and the effect of righteousness quietness and assurance forever" (Isaiah 32:17). However, we have to make sure that this peace is heavenly peace not earthly, human peace. Heavenly peace that makes us feel God's presence more and more strongly.

5. The strengthening of our faith and the liberty in spirit that we receive overcoming all fear and anxiety. For instance, when the apostle Paul was sure of God's perfect will regarding his going to Jerusalem, he was determined to go there in spite of the prophesy of Agabus that he would be bound and put into chains in Jerusalem (Acts 21:11–14).

6. The fulfillment of some sign that we may be constrained to request from God, as Abraham's servant did (Genesis 24:10–21). When the circumstances justify it, we may ask God for some sign to be fulfilled in confirming His perfect will.

7. Full assurance we receive in our hearts that the Lord's name is going to be glorified through the particular matter about which we are seeking to know His perfect will.

Selected Bibliography

Appasamy, A. J. *Sunder Singh: A Biography.* Madras, 1966.

———. *A Bishop's Story.* Madras, 1969.

Azariah, Bishop V. S. *The Shadow of the Mahatma.*

Baago, Kaj. *Pioneers of Indigenous Christianity.* Madras, 1969.

———. *The Discovery of India's Past and Its Effect on the Christian Church in India, in History, and Contemporary India.* Ed. J. C. B. Webster. London, 1971.

Billington, Susan, *The Travails of Christianity in British India.* Harper

Brown, Leslie W. *The Indian Christians of St. Thomas: An Account of the Ancient Syrian Church of Malabar.* Cambridge, 1956, 1982.

Caplan, Lyonel, "The Popular Culture of Evil in Urban South India," *The Anthropology of Evil.* Ed. D. J. Parkin, New York, 1985.

Carre, E. G. *Praying Hyde: Apostle of Prayer.* North Brunswick, N.J: Bridge-Logos Publishers, 1999.

Clark, W.H. *The Oxford Group—Its History and Significance.* Walter Huston. New York: Bookman Associates, 1951.

Collins, Larry, and Dominique Lapierre. *Freedom at Midnight.* New York: Simon & Schuster, 1975.

Din, Lai. *What God Can Do!* Binghamton, NY: Niles and Phipps, 1975.

D'Souza, Herman. *In the Steps of St. Thomas.* Madras, Mylapore, 1983.

Frady, Marshall. *Billy Graham: A Parable of American Righteousness.* Boston: Little, Brown and Company, 1979.

George, P. V. *Unique Christ and Mystic Gandhi.*

George, S. K. *Gandhi's Challenge to Christianity.* Ahmedabad, 1960.

Graham, Billy. *Just as I Am: The Autobiography of Billy Graham.* San Francisco: Harper Collins Worldwide, 1984.

Grant, John Webster. *God's People in India.* Toronto: The Ryerson Press, 1959.

Grubb, Norman. *Once Caught, No Escape: My Life Story.* Fort Washington, PA: Christian Literature Crusade, n.d.

Harper, Susan Billington. *In the Shadow of the Mahatma.* Grand Rapids: William B. Eerdmans Publishing Company, 2000.

Hedlund, Roger E. *Christianity Is Indian: The Emergence of an Indigenous Community.* Kashmere Gate, Delhi: Cambridge Press, 2000.

Hedlund, Roger E. *Quest for Identity (India's Churches of Indigenous Origin: The "Little Tradition" in Indian Christianity).* Kashmere Gate, Delhi: Cambridge Press, 2000.

Hewat, Elizabeth G. K. *Vision and Achievement (1796–1956): A History of the Foreign Missions of the Churches United in the Church of Scotland.* London: Thomas Nelson and Sons, 1960.

Hunt, Dave. *God of the Untouchables.* Old Tappan, NJ: Fleming H. Revell Company, 1976.

Jones, E. Stanley. *The Christ of the Indian Road.* London: Hodder and Stoughton, 1925.

Keay, John. *India: A History.* New York: Grove Press, 2000.

Keer, Dhananjay. *Dr. Ambedkar: Life and Mission.* 3rd ed., Bombay, 1971.

Kinnear, Angus. *The Story of Watchman Nee: Against the Tide.* Wheaton, IL: Tyndale House Publishers, 1982.

Kuriacose, M. K., ed. *History of Christianity in India: Source Materials.* Madras, 1982.

Martin, William. A *Prophet with Honor: The Billy Graham Story.* New York: Quill, 1991.

Murray, Iain H. *David Martin Lloyd-Jones: The First Forty Years (1899–1939).* Edinburgh: Banner of Truth Trust, 1983.

Neill, Stephen C. *A History of Christianity in India 1707–1858.* Cambridge, 1985.

Newbigin, Lesslie. *The Gospel in a Pluralist Society.* Grand Rapids: William B. Eerdmans Publishing Company, 1989.

Orr, J. Edwin. *Evangelical Awakenings in Southern Asia.* Minneapolis: Bethany Fellowship, 1975.

Pollock, J. C. *Earth's Remotest End.* New York: Macmillan Company, 1961.

Rajamani, R. R. *Monsoon Daybreak.* London: Open Books, 1971.

Rajshekar, V. T. *Ambedkar and His Conversion.* Bangalore: Dalit Sahitya Academy, 1983.

———. *Apartheid in India: An International Problem.* Bangalore: Dalit Sahitya Academy, 1983.

———. *The Dilemma Of The Class And Caste.* Bangalore: Dalit Sahitya Academy, 1984.

———. *A Guide to Every Intelligent Indian: Hinduism, Fascism, and Gandhism.* Bangalore: Dalit Sahitya Academy, 1985.

———. *Dalit: The Black Untouchables of India.* Atlanta: Clarity Press, 1995.

Singh, Bakht. *Behold I Will Do a New Thing.* Hyderabad, India: Bakht Singh, 1973.

———. *Bethany.* Bombay, India: Gospel Literature Service, 1971.

———. *Come Let Us Build.* Hyderabad, India: Hebron, 1975.

———. *David Recovered All.* Bombay, India: Gospel Literature Service, 1967.

———. *Divine Principles for a Happy Married Life.* Hyderabad, India: Bakht Singh, 1980.

———. *Forty Mountain Peaks.* Bombay, India: Gospel Literature Service, 1971.

———. *Fullness Of God.* Hyderabad, India: Hebron, 1972.

———. *God's Dwelling Place.* Bombay: Gospel Literature Service, 1957.

———. *Greatest Secret.* Hyderabad, India: Hebron, 1975.

———. *Highway to Victory.* Hyderabad, India: Bakht Singh, 1972.

———. *Holy Spirit.* Bombay, India: Gospel Literature Service, 1970.

———. *How I Got Joy Unspeakable and Full of Glory.* Hyderabad, India: Hebron, 1984.

———. *The Joy of the Lord.* Bombay, India: Gospel Literature Service, 1958.

———. *Looking unto Jesus.* Hyderabad, India: Hebron, 1971.

———. *Much Business.* Hyderabad, India: Hebron, 1984.

———. *My Chosen.* Bombay, India: Gospel Literature Service, 1964.

———. *Our Inheritance.* Hyderabad, India: Hebron, 1974.

———. *The Overcomer's Secret.* Bombay, India: Gospel Literature Service, 1972.

———. *Perfect Security.* Hyderabad, India: Hebron, 1978.

———. *The Return of God's Glory.* Bombay, India: Gospel Literature Service, 1969.

———. *Seven Heavenly Things.* Hyderabad, India: Hebron, 1979.

———. *Sharing God's Secrets.* Bombay, India: Gospel Literature Service, 1982.

———. *Strong Foundation.* Hyderabad, India: Hebron, 1983.

———. *True Liberty.* Hyderabad, India: Hebron, 1976.

———. *True Salt.* Bombay, India: Gospel Literature Service, 1973.

———. *Unsearchable Greatness of Salvation.* Hyderabad, India: Hebron, 1984.

———. *The Voice of the Lord.* Bombay, India: Gospel Literature Service, 1970.

————. *Walk before Me.* Bombay, India: Gospel Literature Service, 1970.

————. *Write the Vision.* Unpublished manuscripts, 1966.

————. *Hebron Messengers.* 1963–1990 (Newsletter).

Smith, Daniel. *Bakht Singh of India: A Prophet of God.* Washington, D.C: International Students Press, n.d.

Yogi, Beulah. *A Soul's Travail Satisfied.* Janpath, New Delhi: Masihi Sahitya Sanstha, 2001.